EFFICIENT C

Thomas Plum
Plum Hall Inc

Jim Brodie
Motorola Microsystems

Plum Hall Inc
1 Spruce Avenue
Cardiff New Jersey 08232

Library of Congress Cataloging in Publication Data

Plum, Thomas, 1943-
  Efficient C.

  Bibliography: p. 10-1.
  Includes index.
  1. C(Computer program language)
I. Brodie, Jim, 1953-   . II. Title.
QA76.73.C15P573 1985   005.13'3   85-45157
ISBN 0-911537-05-8

Acknowledgement of trademarks: UNIX is a trademark of AT&T Bell Laboratories; PDP-11 and VAX are trademarks of Digital Equipment Corporation; CP/M is a trademark of Digital Research Corporation; Venix is a trademark of VenturCom, Inc.; Xenix and MS-DOS are trademarks of Microsoft Corporation; Lattice is a trademark of Lattice, Inc.; Idris is a trademark of Whitesmiths, Ltd.; Tplus is a trademark of Textware International; System V/68 and MC68000 are trademarks of Motorola Inc. C is not a trademark, nor are the names of the software development commands such as cc.

We wish to thank Addison-Wesley Publishing Company for permission to reproduce excepts from copyrighted material:

> *Software Tools in Pascal,* by Brian W. Kernighan and P. J. Plauger, Copyright © by Bell Telephone Laboratories, Inc., and Whitesmiths, Ltd.

ISBN 0-911537-05-8

10 9 8 7 6 5 4 3

This book was set by the authors, using a Hewlett-Packard LaserJet controlled by the Textware Tplus output driver, formatted by troff under the Venix version of the UNIX operating system on a PDP-11/23.

For Joan and Sarah

PREFACE

The C language supplies an effective alternative to assembly language for programmers who are concerned about writing efficient programs. The problem is knowing how to take full advantage of the language and its features to accomplish this task. In this book, we will present the tools and techniques necessary to measure, estimate, and write efficient C programs in your particular environment. These tools and techniques will allow you to customize your program so that you can take advantage of the strengths and avoid the weaknesses of the compiler and machine with which you are working.

Efficiency remains a very important issue in many program development areas. C has the potential to be a very valuable tool for programmers who work in these areas. It is our hope that this book will help strengthen and improve the usefulness of the C tool for programmers who are concerned with generating efficient code.

This book originated with a course on C efficiency which Plum Hall wrote for Bell Laboratories in 1979. Our thanks to Cheron Gelber and Paul Matthews, who supervised the writing of that course, and to Chaim Schaap for many technical contributions, including the bitcnt example and much of the original timing work.

We are indebted to Jon Bentley for his lucid writings on efficiency. We also thank Whitesmiths Ltd., Lattice Inc., AT&T Bell Laboratories, and Motorola Microsystems for the compilers and systems software which we used in the various examples.

For careful reading of the drafts of this book and for other valuable assistance we acknowledge Tim Cwik, Jim D'Ottavi, Steve Hersee, Rex Jaeschke, Christopher Skelly, P. J. Plauger, and Sam Yanuck.

To the staff of Plum Hall Inc — Linda Deutsch, Suzanne Battista, Cathy Bertino, and Anne Hall — our thanks for all the careful work which made possible the writing of this book.

And finally, to Joan Hall and to Sarah Brodie, our thanks for everything.

CONTENTS

INTRODUCTION

We address two kinds of efficiency. The first is the speed of the code generated by the C compiler; this is *time efficiency*. The second is the size of the executable code and data generated from the C program; this is *space efficiency*.

Our main thesis is that one can write efficient C programs without giving up clarity or portability. To this end, we provide a number of tools to assist programmers in estimating and measuring the efficiency of programs, without resorting to assembler listings.

We concentrate on the things that can be said about C programs in any environment; we do not deal with system-specific issues such as operating system throughput, disk speed, and file access times. The system-specific issues are important to the overall functioning of a program within a system; however, very little can be said which applies across the wide range of systems on which C is currently available.

0.1 Why A Book on C Efficiency

Notwithstanding the increasing speed of computers, the increasing sizes of memory, and the decreasing costs of memory, the question of efficiency is still important in most C applications. Experience shows that no matter how powerful a system or how large the available memory, there is a need, in many applications, to use the available resources efficiently.

In programs which interact with a user, such as operating systems and system utilities, response time and system size are almost always significant concerns. Improved efficiency allows the system to handle more users or more tasks in less time.

Device driver and controller applications frequently have response time limitations (e.g., they must respond to an interrupt within 500 microseconds or they lose the data). Many control applications (e.g., systems dedicated to engine control or handling communications protocols on a network) also have severe memory limitations. The cost of not fitting into the available memory can be very high. Frequently, the addition of memory is either not possible (due to the limited address space) or very expensive (in some cases almost doubling the cost of the total control system).

Efficiency is also the concern of many user applications which require large amounts of computing power (e.g., graphics applications). Inefficient use of the available resources can often limit the usefulness of a program by degrading the response time or by requiring a faster processor or larger memory to run effectively. This is of particular concern in the development of applications which will run on personal computers or engineering work stations. In these environments, applications are often pushing the computing power to the limit, trying to do mainframe work on a microprocessor.

In these types of applications, as well as in general programming, C is frequently the language of choice. There are several reasons for this choice.

C is a low level language which gives considerable control over the generated machine code. The language has features, such as the register specifier and bit fields, which allow the tailoring of programs by telling the C compiler how to most effectively use the resources of the hardware. Further, the C language has been designed to map in a relatively straightforward way onto most of today's computers.

C also gives considerable freedom to manipulate data at a lower, more detailed level than is provided in most high level languages. This allows "bit twiddling" and other machine-oriented things when they are the best way to get the job done. C allows the programmer to stay close to the hardware while retaining the advantages of a higher level language, including control flow constructs (if-else, loops, etc.), data structuring features (structures, unions, arrays, etc.), and support for modular programming (functions and separate compilation).

In a very real sense, C is a user-optimizable language. C gives the control and the responsibility for tailoring the code for an application to the user. This book gives the programmer the tools and techniques necessary to be effective in the role of optimizer.

C also allows the development of portable programs. Since C compilers are available on many different systems, programs can be developed which need to run in a wide variety of environments. We hope that our empirical approach to C efficiency will encourage the development of programs that are portable as well as efficient.

0.2 Overview of the Book

Chapter 1 describes the four environments that we used for our timing experiments. We then carry a small C function through four stages of optimization. At each stage, we estimate how much time the new version will take, and measure the actual timing improvement.

Chapter 2 describes several techniques for measuring the execution time of programs and of individual expressions. By presenting actual execution-time figures for operators, control structures, and functions, we provide the information that is needed to make rough estimates of the time that a particular algorithm will take, as well as the intuition needed to evaluate the effect of changing data types or adding a floating-point processor to the system.

Chapter 3 discusses when and how to make execution time estimates before writing the code. We then summarize generally-known techniques for improving the time efficiency of a program, whether or not it is in C.

Chapter 4 discusses the efficiency techniques that are more specific to C: optimizations done by the compiler, using the most efficient data size, register storage, fast loops, macros, and pointers. We then discuss the use of a profiler to determine where optimizations may still be needed.

In Chapter 5 we turn to the measurement of memory space for program and data. We discuss how to measure the requirements for program space, static data space, and dynamic data space.

Chapter 6 discusses techniques for estimating space requirements in advance of the programming. Again, different techniques are needed for program space, static data space, and dynamic data space.

Chapter 7 offers suggestions for improving space efficiency: register variables, small data types, bit packing, unions, arrays vs linked data structures, dynamic vs static allocation, controlling the growth of the stack, and using a function to represent data.

Chapter 8 describes the techniques that you might use in translating a program written in some other language into efficient C.

The Appendix gives the listings of the timing software that you can use to time operators and statements in your own environment, plus various notes of interest mainly to compiler implementers.

We begin with a simple example.

CHAPTER 1: A SIMPLE EXAMPLE

In designing your code for efficiency, you will need to be able to make intuitive estimates about the speed of the important parts of your algorithm. When you suspect that a part of your program may be too slow, you can often improve its performance by a factor of two or three with techniques described in this book. But in order to know which techniques to try, you need to have some intuition about where the algorithm is spending its time. To help you develop this intuition, we will present relevant empirical information from a series of timing experiments.

In this chapter, we will carry a simple example through a series of optimizations. Each time we program a version of the example, we will estimate how much time we think that it will take. Then when we run the example and get its actual timing, we can see how close our estimate is. The estimates — crude as they are — turn out to be within 30% of the true figure every time, and usually much closer. With the ability to make reasonably close estimates of execution time, we can often determine — on a real problem — whether it is worth re-programming an algorithm to obtain more speed.

We needed to be sure that our experiments were representative of a wide range of typical environments, so we selected four different compilers for four different machines.

1.1 Representative Environments

Our representative environments ranged from a small microprocessor with an 8-bit data path (the 8088) to a super-minicomputer with a 32-bit data path (the VAX-11/780). On the IBM PC/Intel 8088 we used the Lattice compiler (version 2.15). On the PDP-11 we used the Whitesmiths compiler (version 2.3). On the Motorola 68000 we used the compiler of the System V/68 version of UNIX. And on the VAX 11/780 we also used the VAX UNIX System V compiler. Each of these environments can be characterized by several parameters:

	8088/PC Lattice	PDP-11/23 WSL	MC68000 V/68	VAX-11/780 UNIX V
Size of int	16 bits	16 bits	32 bits	32 bits
Width of data path	8 bits	16 bits	16 bits	32 bits
Machine clock rate	(std)	(std)	10 MHz	(std)
Memory wait states	-	-	1	-
Avg C op (usec)	8.77	13.5	4.73	1.85
Avg fn call (1 arg)	39.0	73.4	18.1	20.4

Our results were generally consistent across all environments. If you are using one of these environments, our figures are likely to be directly applicable. If you are working in a different environment, you can use our figures for general guidelines, and apply our specific measurement tools to get similar figures for your own environment.

The "average C operator" is the average of an assortment of operations upon short int data. We will use these figures in the examples of this chapter. Similarly, the "average function call" is an average time to call a function with one argument and to return. Such figures are, of course, extreme simplifications. (For technical details of interest mostly to compiler implementers, occasional references to the appendix will be specified with bold note-numbers [1-1].) As we shall see, such simplifications turn out to be very useful for estimating the execution time for a given algorithm. The method of deriving the averages and the specific timings will be described in Chapter 2.

1.2 An Example

As an example of the kind of evaluation and optimization which can be done, let us look at a small function. We will concentrate on time efficiency in this simple example. The function, named bitcnt, counts the number of bits which are "set" (i.e., equal to 1) in a byte-sized argument. Our first try at this function is shown below. It takes the straightforward, brute force approach of shifting each bit into the low order position and then ANDing with a 1 to determine if that bit has been set. It keeps a counter, b, of the number of times that the AND successfully matches a 1 bit.

Note that CHAR_BIT is a constant, defined before the function, which holds the number of bits in a char variable. (The first line of each program example, such as "bitcnt(#1):" below, is an example-name title, not part of the program.)

```
bitcnt(#1):
    /*  bitcnt - return the bit sum of a byte argument
     *  version 1
     */
    #define CHAR_BIT 8
    int bitcnt(c)
        char c;
        {
        int b;
        int i;

        b = 0;
        for (i = 0; i < CHAR_BIT; ++i)
            if (((c >> i) & 01) != 0)
                ++b;
        return (b);
        }
```

The following table presents the timing results in our four environments. Each column describes one environment, showing the "estimated" time, the "actual" time, and the percent of error in the estimate:

	8088/PC Lattice	PDP-11/23 WSL	MC68000 V/68	VAX-11/780 UNIX V
Avg C op (usec)	8.77	13.5	4.73	1.85
Avg fn call (1 arg)	39.0	73.4	18.1	20.4
bitcnt V1 (estim.)	442.	692.	236.	105.5
bitcnt V1 (actual)	411.	455.	189.	86.9
estim. error (%)	7%	34%	20%	18%

Let us use the first column as representative of the others. Using our "average operation" and "average function" figures, we estimated that this function would take 442 microseconds (millionths of a second) to execute on an 8088 using the code generated from the Lattice compiler (version 2.15). Briefly, this timing estimate is based on several factors. We estimate that the "average C operator" takes approximately 8.77 microseconds in this environment. Next we look at the number of operators and the number of times they will be executed. Considering first the main loop of the program, the <, >>, &, !=, and ++ (in ++i) operators are done each time through the loop. The ++ (in ++b) will (on the average) be done one half of the time. The number of operations in the loop is the number of operators (5.5) times the number of times through the loop (8). There are also two operators outside the loop, for a total of 46. The average function call and return time is 39.0 microseconds in this environment, so 46 times 8.77 plus 39.0 gives 442 (to three figures).

An actual timing, using a byte with 4 bits set as input (0143) gave us a measured CPU time of 411 microseconds. The estimated and actual times are within 7% of each other in this case. At this level of crude estimation, we would be satisfied with agreements to within a factor of two. The close agreement is merely coincidental. Throughout this chapter, the error percentage ranged from practically nothing to almost 50%, so from now on we will focus on the improvement between each version, rather than on the error percentage. We are, after all, using very rough "average operator" figures. Furthermore, as we will see in Chapter 4, the compilers can give us better-than-average code for certain special cases, such as comparison against zero, so we would expect our estimates to err on the high side.

We now begin to look for ways to improve the speed of this function. On many machines, shifts by one bit are faster than multi-bit shifts. In reviewing the function to incorporate this change we also observe that we can eliminate the need for the loop counter i. We can modify the value we are looking at so that we will end up with a zero value after we have seen all of the 1-bits.

```
bitcnt(#2):
    /*  bitcnt - return the bit sum of a byte argument
     *  version 2
     */
    #define BYTEMASK 0xFF
    int bitcnt(c)
        char c;
        {
        int b;
        unsigned uc;

        uc = c & BYTEMASK;
        b = 0;
        while (uc != 0)
            {
            if ((uc & 01) != 0)
                ++b;
            uc >>= 1;
            }
        return (b);
        }
```

The new function takes the argument value, masks it to avoid possible sign-extension, and then proceeds to loop until there are no bits set in the word.

Each time through the loop, the low order bit is ANDed with 1, just as was done in our first version. However, now the value is shifted to the right, discarding the low order bit and filling the high order bit with a 0. This modified value is then used in the next iteration through the loop.

Using the same approach as before we can estimate how long this version of bitcnt will take to execute:

	8088/PC Lattice	PDP-11/23 WSL	MC68000 V/68	VAX-11/780 UNIX V
Avg C op (usec)	8.77	13.5	4.73	1.85
Avg fn call (1 arg)	39.0	73.4	18.1	20.4
bitcnt V2 (estim.)	341.	539.	181.	84.3
bitcnt V2 (actual)	292.	305.	143.	79.1
estim. error (%)	14%	43%	20%	6%
improvement over V1	29%	33%	24%	9%

Following the second column this time (PDP-11/23), the operators require, on average, 13.5 microseconds. The !=, &, !=, and >>= operators are done each time through the loop. (The >>= assignment operator could be counted as more than one operator. Still, it has fewer loads and stores than two separate operators, so we kept the simple treatment.) The ++ is done, on average, one half of the time.

The number of times through the loop is now data-dependent. On average, we will go through the loop 7 times. (This is derived by observing that 1/2 of the time 8 iterations through the loop will be required, 1/4 of the time 7 iterations, 1/8 of the time 6 iterations, etc.) The estimate of the execution time is 539 microseconds:

(7 * 4.5 + 3) * 13.5 + 73.4 = 539.

An actual timing, using the byte set to 0143 as input, gave us a measured CPU time of 305 microseconds. This is about a 33 percent improvement over our first version.

The next optimization uses one of the C language features, the register storage class specifier. This feature tells the compiler that a variable will be used heavily. As a general rule, the specification of the the register storage class on key variables will improve execution efficiency. It is also guaranteed to be safe and harmless, provided (of course) that the program does not take the address of those variables. In our third version of bitcnt, we make uc and b register variables:

```
bitcnt(#3):
    /*  bitcnt - return the bit sum of a byte argument
     *  version 3
     */
    #define BYTEMASK 0xFF
    int bitcnt(c)
        register char c;
        {
        register int b;
        register unsigned uc;

        uc = c & BYTEMASK;
        b = 0;
        while (uc != 0)
            {
            if ((uc & 01) != 0)
                b++;
            uc >>= 1;
            }
        return (b);
        }
```

One rule of thumb, which was developed by looking at execution timings, says that 68000 register operations are about one-third faster. Looking at the third column (68000), the "average operation" time has dropped from 4.73 to 2.61 microseconds. Using the method described in the previous version we estimate the execution time to be 108 microseconds:

	8088/PC Lattice	PDP-11/23 WSL	MC68000 V/68	VAX-11/780 UNIX V
Avg C op (usec)	8.77	8.31	2.61	1.30
Avg fn call (1 arg)	39.0	73.4	18.1	20.4
bitcnt V3 (estim.)	341.	359.	108.	65.2
bitcnt V3 (actual)	292.	234.	86.2	61.9
estim. error (%)	14%	35%	20%	5%
improvement over V1	29%	49%	52%	29%

An actual timing, using the byte set to 0143 as input, gave us a measured CPU time of 86.2 microseconds. This is about a 40 percent improvement from the previous version, and about a 52 percent improvement over the original version.

Notice that the times in the first column are the same for versions two and three. The Lattice 2.15 compiler ignores the programmer's specification of register storage, and instead allocates registers as it thinks best. On these small examples, most loop variables will be kept in machine registers by a compiler such as this, so there would be little difference between ordinary and register timings.

The optimization that has been done so far is called *local optimization*, since it has not changed the basic structure of the algorithm or data. If local optimizations do not yield the necessary improvement then a more radical approach is needed: the user must look for a more effective algorithm or data structure. This approach, known as *global optimization*, is often the most effective way to improve performance.

In our bitcnt example, the idea behind a better algorithm comes from a comment in Kernighan and Ritchie [1978]. They note that "in a 2's complement number system, x & (x-1) deletes the rightmost 1 bit in x." (Actually, this is true for positive numbers in any binary system.)

```
    x       bbb...bbb10000
    x-1     bbb...bbb01111

  x & (x-1) bbb...bbb00000
```

Using this idea as the seed, a new approach can be taken to bitcnt:

```
bitcnt(#4):
    /*  bitcnt - return the bit sum of a byte argument
     *  version 4
     */
    #define BYTEMASK 0xFF
    int bitcnt(c)
        register char c;
        {
        register int b;
        register unsigned uc;

        uc = c & BYTEMASK;
        b = 0;
        while (uc != 0)
            {
            b++;
            uc &= uc - 1;
            }
        return b;
        }
```

Each time through the `while` loop, we turn off the rightmost 1-bit in our variable `uc`. Now we will only go through the loop once for each bit which is set, no matter where the bits occur in the byte.

On average there will be four bits set in a byte so there will be four iterations through the loop. Each iteration uses four operators, so our crude estimate is sixteen operations in the inner loop, plus three operations outside the loop. Looking at the fourth column (VAX 11/780) this time, the time estimate is 45.1 microseconds:

	8088/PC Lattice	PDP-11/23 WSL	MC68000 V/68	VAX-11/780 UNIX V
Avg C op (usec)	8.77	8.31	2.61	1.30
Avg fn call (1 arg)	39.0	73.4	18.1	20.4
bitcnt V4 (estim.)	204.	231.	67.7	45.1
bitcnt V4 (actual)	200.	162.	59.0	39.6
estim. error (%)	2%	29%	13%	12%
improvement over V1	51%	64%	69%	54%

An actual timing, using a byte set to 0143 as input, gave us a measured CPU time of 39.6 microseconds.

Through this series of optimizations we have reduced the actual execution time of this function to less than half of its original value. With some confidence in the rough accuracy of the timing estimates, we could use this type of estimate to determine whether a proposed optimization will actually produce a worthwhile result.

In the succeeding chapters, we will investigate techniques which will yield still greater optimizations of the `bitcnt` operation.

1.3 Some Caveats to the Reader

At this point it is useful to give a couple of words of caution. There is an old adage, "make it right before you make it fast." This is good advice. Correctness should not be sacrificed for speed. You should not spend time doing optimizations unless you know that they will pay off. However, understanding the issues related to efficiency will allow you to develop programs which are both correct and efficient.

The techniques described in this book allow you to evaluate the compiler you are currently using. If you make use of them to time code samples on your system, you can be sure that the figures you use are exactly relevant. There is, after all, no guarantee that the next release of your C compiler or the next machine you move to will have the same characteristics.

We will demonstrate characteristics across a variety of machines and compilers. This will provide a basis for generalizations about the kind of C program constructs which will usually generate efficient code by C compilers. The generalizations represent averages and tendencies, not universal rules.

The real strength of this book is the tools it supplies, and the most benefit will come to those who use these tools in their work.

CHAPTER 2: MEASURING TIME

If we are to avoid passing on obsolete superstition about what is efficient and what is not, then we must have tools to measure our programs. We will start by looking at the tools and techniques which are available to evaluate the time efficiency of our programs.

2.1 Cycle Counting

The most basic approach to determining how long a program will take is to count the machine cycles used by the code which is generated from the C code. This is done by using a processor or assembler manual and inspecting either the assembly language generated by the compiler (if this is actually generated and can be made available) or the disassembled object (if a disassembler is available).

Although this is a tedious process, it is usually the most accurate way of measuring the time which will be required to execute a piece of code.

This is the only approach which can be used on systems where it is not possible to actually time the execution of the code (e.g., some controller environments). However, the usefulness of this approach is not limited to these types of systems. Applications which are under severe time limitations, such as device controllers and interrupt handlers, may require this type of timing on almost any machine.

This approach is also useful on any machine where the timing must be more accurate than that supplied by the system timing facilities.

There are some limitations to the cycle counting approach.

It has the obvious disadvantage of requiring that you actually review assembly language and that you gain a great deal of familiarity with the instruction set and addressing modes of the machine on which the code will run. In some applications this may be appropriate but usually the high level language programmer does not want to deal with the machine at this very low level.

It also may not be a simple task to get the assembly language. This is particularly true when the compiler generates load modules directly, rather than going through assembly language. Even if a disassembler is available, problems may arise when trying to disassemble code which contains embedded constant data values in the the code space.

On machines with pipelining or cache memory, the actual timings may depend on factors other than just the generated assembly language. Factors such as the cache hit rate and the instruction mix may affect the actual timings when the code is executed.

2.2 Timing Executing Programs

Most applications do not require the accuracy that is supplied by the cycle counting approach to timing. In these cases, when a clock and some way to determine timings is available, timings can be done by actually executing the generated code for the operations.

Some larger systems supply a facility which reports how long it takes to execute a program. In the UNIX family, this command is called the time command.

The time command produces three numbers associated with the execution of a program: *real time, system time,* and *user time*. The real time is the elapsed "wall clock time" (in other words, the total time from the start to finish of the program). Since UNIX is a multi-tasking system, this includes all of the time used by this program and any other programs which were executing during the same period of time. On multi-tasking systems the real time varies widely depending on the loading of the system. It is not, in general, an accurate way to evaluate a program although it may be valuable for getting a "general feel" for the execution time for the program on a loaded system.

The user time is a UNIX estimate of how much time the CPU was dedicated to executing the user's program. The system time is a UNIX estimate of how much time the operating system spent servicing requests from the user program (e.g., I/O requests).

The combination of user time plus system time is the accumulated CPU time which was "charged" to the program during its execution. This is the UNIX estimate of how much of the processor time was dedicated to user program rather than other tasks which were running during the same period of time.

On single user systems which do not supply a timing utility, a stopwatch can be used to time the running of a program. The timing is taken from the point where the program is initiated (on most systems this is the moment of hitting carriage return) until the prompt is given indicating that the next program can be executed.

On multi-user systems which do not supply some form of time command you should do stopwatch timings when there are no other users on the system so that the results are a close approximation of the time that the system actually spent working on the program.

We can use the simple technique of timing an executable program to determine how long it takes to execute individual operators (e.g., +, /) or statements (e.g., for, if). This ability to time operators and statements lays the foundation for making accurate estimates of how long various algorithms or processes will take.

Let's take a first try at determining how long the long divide takes to execute on the PDP 11/23 running Whitesmiths 2.3 Idris C compiler. The execution of a single divide operation is too fast to accurately time, so we will build a loop to execute the divide instruction 10,000 times:

```
harness1.c:
    /* harness1 - execute repetitive long division */
    #define LOOPCNT 10000
    main()
        {
        long a, b = 255, c = 255, i;

        for (i = 1; i <= LOOPCNT; ++i)
            a = b / c;
        }
```

When we time this program, using the time command, we get a result of 12.00 seconds of real time, 11.15 seconds of user time, and 0.08 seconds of system time. Notice how close the sum of the user time and system time is to real time. We had the machine all to ourselves.

If you review this program, you can see that we are timing a great deal more than simply the divide instruction. We are including all of the program startup and shutdown time, the time for the for loop, and the time for the assignment instruction.

The first step to handling this problem of program timing over-head is to subtract out all of the time which is not associated with the divide instruction. This can be done by timing the program, including the loop and the assignment statement, but without the divide opera-tion. (We are assuming an "additivity" of times for portions of the C program [2-1].) The modified program, known as a timing harness, looks like this:

```
harness2.c:
    /* harness2 - execute repetitive loop */
    #define LOOPCNT 10000
    main()
        {
        long a, b = 255, c = 255, i;

        for (i = 1; i <= LOOPCNT; ++i)
            a = b;        /* simple assignment statement */
        }
```

We only need to get an accurate time for the harness once. After that, it is only necessary to time the programs with the operation added appropriately. The results of the execution are 1.00 seconds of real time, 0.38 seconds of user time, and 0.07 seconds of system time.

The time required for the timing harness is subtracted from the timing value which was obtained from the the complete program. This results in the time which can be attributed to the divide operator. When we divide this by 10,000 we get our estimate for each divide instruction:

```
(11.15 - .38) seconds * 1000000 usec/sec / 10000 iterations = 1067 usec
```

There are several limitations of this approach to timing operators or statements. The first limitation is that we can time only one operator at a time. In addition, it requires either that the system supply a timing command or that we use the tedious stopwatch method. This is a seri-ous limitation since many systems, including MS-DOS, have no time command equivalent. In the next sections we will explore techniques for overcoming these limitations.

2.3 Timing Parts of a Program

If a function call to obtain the current system time is available on a system and there is a way to access it from a C program, then a slightly different approach can be taken which avoids the above problems. Using this facility we can build a framework for testing a series of operators within a single program.

To isolate the system dependencies we built a function, called cputim, which returns the accumulated time since the last call to cputim. This routine will take care of the particulars of obtaining the system time and doing the appropriate calculations. The value that it returns is a long integer that counts some fundamental "clock tick" for each environment. The header cputim.h declares the cputim function and defines a constant named CLOCK_TICKS_PER_SECOND.

Beyond this, the internal details of cputim are irrelevant to the timing process. The appendix has a complete listing of the cputim functions which were used in the timings for the four example systems used in this book [2-2].

We can now bracket individual timing loops with calls to cputim. The following example shows the use of this approach to time a long divide and a long add. (We increased the iterations to 100,000 to get a more accurate estimate.)

```
harness3.c:
    /* harness3 - time long divide and long add */
    #include <stdio.h>
    #include "cputim.h"

    #define LOOPCNT 100000

    main()
        {
        double time0, timediv, timeadd;
        long a, b = 255, c = 255, i;

        cputim();  /* time the timing harness */
        for (i = 1; i <= LOOPCNT; ++i)
            a = b;
        time0 = cputim() * (1e6 / CLOCK_TICKS_PER_SECOND);

        cputim();  /* time the divide operator */
        for (i = 1; i <= LOOPCNT; ++i)
            a = b / c;
        timediv = cputim() * (1e6 / CLOCK_TICKS_PER_SECOND);

        cputim();  /* time the addition operator */
        for (i = 1; i <= LOOPCNT; ++i)
            a = b + c;
        timeadd = cputim() * (1e6 / CLOCK_TICKS_PER_SECOND);

        printf("long divides require %.1f microseconds \n",
            (timediv - time0)/LOOPCNT);
        printf("long additions require %.1f microseconds \n",
            (timeadd - time0)/LOOPCNT);
        }
```

On the PDP-11/23, harness3 produced this output:

```
harness3.out:
    long divides require 1061.5 microseconds
    long additions require 16.7 microseconds
```

There are several ways in which this approach can be improved. The
timing loop is especially inefficient on small machines, because the loop
counter is long (to allow for the large number of executions) and long
arithmetic tends to be slow on small machines. We cannot just replace
the long variable with an int (or a short) because of the large number of
iterations. We could still preserve portability if we used two nested
loops with int loop counters. For example, assume that we initialize
t_majrlim to 100, and t_minrlim to 1000, and then execute a loop like this:

```
for (t_major = 1; t_major <= t_majrlim; ++t_major)
    for (t_minor = 1; t_minor <= t_minrlim; ++t_minor)
        code sample being timed
```

There is, in fact, an even more efficient form for each loop, as we will see in Section 4.4. A more fundamental problem is that the simple harness does not test to see whether the timed code exceeds the basic harness time by an amount sufficient to produce a reliable result. We determined that the sample time had to exceed the harness time by an amount t_minsam (chosen for each environment) so that the sample was sufficient for one percent accuracy. With this augmentation, the overall control flow looks like this:

```
t_reps = 1;
do {
    set t_majrlim and t_minrlim to produce t_reps repetitions;
    time each sample if it has not achieved t_minsam;
    multiply t_reps by 10;
    } while (more to time && t_reps <= T_MAXITER);
```

Finally, these complications deserve some macros to hide the messy details. We create a header called timer1.h which generates all the overall control structure and defines several macros. The DO_IEXPR macro will perform a sample expression enough times to get one percent accuracy (after subtracting the appropriate harness time). The matching macro OD must appear at the end of the sample expression. OD closes some loops and calls some tabulation functions. Because of all the generated control structures, the final source file starts with

```
#include "timer1.h"
```

in place of the usual

```
main()
    {
```

function definition. After all these transformations, our timing software would accept a file that looks like this:

```
ldivadd.c:
    /* ldivadd - time the long divide and long add */
    #include "timer1.h"

        long  b = 255, c = 255;

        DO_IEXPR("long divide")      b / c   OD
        DO_IEXPR("long add")         b + c   OD
    }
```

To summarize: Our timing method makes two assumptions: (1) that the time to perform the code sample is a simple sum of time to execute the harness and time to perform the sampled operation ("additivity of

execution times"); and (2) that the code sample being timed can meaningfully be repeated an arbitrary number of times ("repeatability of
code sample"). If these assumptions are met, then the timing software
described in the appendix will accept source files like ldivadd.c and produce execution-time estimates accurate to one percent [2-3].

2.4 Looking At the Details

At this point we have laid the fundamental groundwork for doing
timings. However, we have glossed over many details, such as how the
operands of an operation affect the time required to do an operation.

To develop a fuller understanding of the timing process we must
now tackle some of the details if we are going to do accurate, repeatable
timings.

We begin by looking at the factors which affect how long a simple
C operation, such as + (addition) or / (division) will take.

The time required for a simple operation depends on three primary factors. The first is the operation to be performed. Most of the
operators supported in C are shown below.

member	s.m	multiply	j * k
member	p->m	divide	j / k
subscript	a[k]	remainder	j % k
casts	(double)k	addition	j + k
	(long)k	subtraction	j - k
	(int)k	left shift	j << k
	(char)k	right shift	j >> k
address	&k	compare	j <= k etc.
bit-negate	~k	equality	j != k j == k
postfix	k++ k--	and	j && k
prefix	++k --k	or	j || k
not	!k	bit-and	j & k
unary minus	-k	bit-or	j | k
		exclusive-or	j ^ k
		conditional	i ? j : k
		assignment	j = k

There can be an order of magnitude or more difference between
the speed of the underlying machine instructions for two operations on
the same machine (e.g., plus and divide on the Motorola 68000).

The second factor is the type of the operands. The base types in C
are:

char	unsigned char	float
short	unsigned short	double
int	unsigned int	
long	unsigned long	

If int is shorter than long, it is usually faster. However, there are cases where operations with short operands take more time than operations with longer operands (e.g., short and int on a VAX). This effect is seen because of the time required to convert the short value to int size before the operation takes place.

The third factor is storage class. In many implementations, automatic variables are referenced in a very different way from static variables. These differences may translate into different addressing modes in the generated instructions and possibly totally different code sequences if the related machine instructions have limitations on the types of addressing modes which can used. The register storage class produces faster and smaller code sequences in many implementations.

In some environments, externally-linked variables (whose names are published to the linker) are accessed differently from internally-linked variables ("file static"), although none of the sample environments behave this way. Note that function arguments are usually referenced in the same way as automatic variables.

The combination of type and storage class produces a multitude of possible operand combinations for each operator.

Fortunately, timing tests are not required for all possible combinations because the combinations reduce to a much smaller set of groups which share common properties. Most C compilers only deal with two lengths of integers. Either short or long variables become the same as int. In most implementations, operations with unsigned operands may be merged with operations with signed variables. On some machines, float and double are reduced to a single type.

In some cases, the effects of data type far outweigh the effects of storage class, so that distinctions of storage class can be ignored. This is usually the case with float and double operations.

Our procedure for determining the relevant factors for each environment was to time fifteen different operators with all relevant combinations of type and storage class, and then to cluster the resulting times into groups whose times differ by no more than 30%. Each of the following tables shows the distinct groups which are of interest in its particular environment.

Timing results on 8088/PC with Lattice 2.15 compiler:

time.88:
    Execution times for operators
    8088/PC Lattice 2.15 MS-DOS
    Small model

Operation	short (1)	char (2)	long (3)	(FPP) double (4)	(no FPP) double (5)
"average"	8.77	10.3	47.	218. a	218. c
s.m	0.0	0.0	0.0	0.0	0.0
p->m	3.34	7.94	3.34		
a[k]	7.94	8.80	7.94		
(double)k	162.	162.	178.	0.0 a	0.0 c
(long)k	6.11	6.88	0.0	348. a	348. c
(int)k	0.0	0.0	0.0	176. a	176. c
(char)k	0.32	0.0	0.32	178. a	178. c
&k		0.0	0.0	0.0	0.0
~k	0.32	1.56	6.88		
++k	4.22	5.55	18.6	203. b	842. d
k++	5.56	14.6	19.8		
!k	6.88	6.11	12.2	140.	140.
-k	0.32	1.57	10.6	26.6 a	26.5 c
j * k	32.7	45.2	857.	187. b	2710. d
j / k	39.8	53.6	650.	209. b	4230. d
j % k	39.8	53.6	650.		
j + k	3.56	6.88	14.6	186. b	753. d
j - k	3.56	6.88	14.6	187. b	674. d
j << k	18.6	22.1	135.		
j >> k	18.6	22.1	135.		
j <= k	11.7	14.6	61.0	309. b	334. d
j != k	12.2	15.4	23.3	233. b	257. d
j && k	11.4	10.0	17.8	195.	240.
j || k	11.4	10.0	17.8	195.	240.
j & k	3.56	6.88	14.6		
j | k	3.56	6.88	14.6		
j ^ k	3.56	6.87	14.6		
i ? j : k	11.8	11.8	20.5	36.0 a	36.1 c
j = k	10.4	7.19	19.9	34.2	34.3

Times are in microseconds (+30%)

(1) short, int, unsigned int (2) char (3) long (4) double, float (no FPP)
(5) double, float (FPP)

Notes: a = add 400 usec for float   b = add 800 usec for float
        c = add 125 usec for float   d = add 250 usec for float

Each of these tables shows the categories that are important for execution speed in its environment. Some machines give different results for different sizes of integers, while others give different results for different storage classes. On some machines, the presence or absence of a floating-point processor (FPP) produces vast differences in the floating-point times.

Our purpose in showing all the detail of these tables is to give you an intuitive feel for the times of operators and their relative speeds. Furthermore, the tables can give you "ball park" figures for the speed that you can expect from your own environment. We ran our timings in four environments to validate our conclusions on a representative sampling of current C compilers. There was no attempt to validate any comparisons of different machines or different software vendors, and we do not wish the figures to be used for "apples vs oranges" comparisons.

Now let us consider this specific table for the Lattice 8088 environment. Most integer operations take a small number of microseconds. Multiply and divide are expensive, relative to other operations on the same types, except for floating-point operations with floating-point processor ("FPP") support (fourth column). The FPP support here is in the form of the 8087 auxiliary chip. Floating-point operations are very expensive when FPP support is not available. Compare the arithmetic operators in the fourth and fifth columns. Most operations upon float operands are slower than the same operations upon double operands, as indicated by the footnotes (a, b, c, d).

Similarly, long multiply, divide, remainder, and shift are disproportionately expensive. This reflects the underlying hardware's lack of 32-bit machine instructions; most long operations must be done via function calls in the generated code.

The address-of (&) and structure member (.) operators take no execution time when the operand is a simple variable. Postfix increment and decrement are slightly more expensive of time when, as in the timing suite, the expression value of the result is used.

Timing results on PDP 11/23 with Whitesmiths 2.3 compiler on Idris:

```
time.23:
    Execution times for operators
    PDP 11/23 Whitesmiths 2.3 Idris
```

Operation	register (1)	short (2)	long (3)	(FPP) double (4)	(no FPP) double (5)
"average"	8.31	13.5	26.8	74.0	1590.
s.m		3.35	3.37		
p->m	5.43	8.72	8.73		
a[k]	9.55	12.9	12.9		
(double)k	2440.	2440.	2450.	2.	0.00
(long)k	4.20	7.63	3.35	62.	985.
(int)k	0.0	3.35	5.53	41.	985.
(char)k	0.0	3.35	5.53	41.	985.
&k		5.80	5.83	6.	5.68
~k	4.18	7.63	15.0		
++k	2.12	10.0	18.3	120.	1050.
k++	4.18	12.1	25.8		
!k	6.28	10.1	24.4	27.	91.8
-k	4.18	8.05	17.1	20.	77.5
j * k	27.3	32.6	972.	227.	5370.
j / k	47.9	53.3	1060.	264.	9370.
j % k	47.8	53.3	1060.		
j + k	4.20	11.2	23.8	80.	884.
j - k	4.18	10.8	23.9	82.	1110.
j << k	21.8	26.9	40.4		
j >> k	24.6	31.3	51.6		
j <= k	9.87	16.6	36.1	88.	2850.
j != k	6.28	13.0	32.1	64.	221.
j && k	11.9	15.1	40.0	64.	2740.
j || k	11.9	15.1	40.0	64.	2740.
j & k	8.37	15.0	30.1		
j | k	4.20	10.8	21.8		
j ^ k	4.20	12.9	25.9		
i ? j : k	8.37	15.0	35.9	31.	46.5
j = k	2.03	9.23	18.6	39.	36.9

```
Times are in microseconds (+30%)

(1) register int
(2) short, unsigned short, int, unsigned int, char, unsigned char
(3) long (4) double, float (with FPP) (5) double, float (no FPP)

Note:   unsigned char: plus, minus  70% slower than char
        unsigned short: divide, >>   behave like  long int
```

Again, most integer operations take a small number of microseconds. Multiply and divide are relatively expensive. Floating-point is especially expensive without FPP support. (Whitesmiths generates completely different code sequences for FPP environments.) There is little penalty for float arithmetic.

Postfix increment and decrement are again somewhat more expensive than the prefix version, when embedded into larger expressions.

The time shown for the (double) cast was timed without FPP support; with FPP support, it would be much faster.

Operands in register storage are processed about one-third faster, on the average. No other effect of storage class was significant.

One important exception is noted at the bottom of the figure: Division and right-shift of unsigned short (i.e., unsigned int) are extremely slow, taking the same time as long operands.

Some points to remember regarding the tables for all the environments: First, the timings for the specific operations shown are accurate to one percent, but each column is representative of several different data types, whose timings are generally within 30% of the timings indicated. (The second column, for example, represents unsigned int as well as ordinary short and int.) Second, the timing of an operation embedded in a larger computation may be faster or slower than the timing of the isolated operation. The figures are intended for rough estimation, not for exact timing.

Timing results on 68000 with System V/68 compiler:

```
time.68k:
    Execution times for operators
    68000 System V/68
    10MHz, 1 wait state
    No floating point processor
```

Operation	register (1)	auto (2)	static (3)	double (4)	float (5)
"average"	2.61	4.73	5.71	107.	135.
s.m		2.15	2.68		
p->m	2.15	4.28	4.80		
a[k]	4.67	6.33	7.45		
(double)k	93.8	95.7	96.2	0.0	29.7
(long)k	0.0	2.13	2.68	67.5	74.1
(int)k	0.0	2.15	2.68	67.5	74.0
(char)k	1.63	2.68	3.23	68.7	75.1
&k		1.63	1.62	1.63	1.64
~k	1.29	2.90	3.37		
++k	0.89	4.28	5.35	114.	220.
k++	1.49	4.27	5.33		
!k	2.33	3.37	3.93	50.7	49.8
-k	1.29	2.90	3.37	9.90	38.5
j * k	36.7	8.27	9.13	240.	305.
j / k	115.	47.8	48.7	485.	552.
j % k	114.	50.2	48.3		
j + k	1.49	5.23	6.28	110.	155.
j - k	1.49	5.23	6.28	121.	146.
j << k	4.58	7.82	8.57		
j >> k	4.60	7.82	8.78		
j <= k	4.07	6.48	7.70	134.	199.
j != k	2.57	5.02	6.07	76.2	141.
j && k	4.72	6.32	7.11	117.	116.
j || k	4.72	6.32	7.11	117.	116.
j & k	1.49	5.22	6.30		
j | k	1.49	5.23	6.28		
j ^ k	1.49	5.23	6.28		
i ? j : k	3.82	7.02	8.12	20.5	78.3
j = k	0.53	2.65	3.75	7.45	4.25

```
Times are in microseconds (+30%)
```

(1) register int (2) auto: long, int, short, char, and unsigned varieties
(3) static: long, int, short, char, and unsigned varieties
(4) double (5) float

Note: unsigned (all): division is 25% faster
        short (signed): multiply is 400% faster

The 68000 has some interestingly different features: The times for all sizes of integer are close enough to be represented by one column, but static storage was enough slower to be worth its own column. In particular, long arithmetic has no penalty, as would be expected from this 32-bit int processor. (One exception: short multiply is much faster.) This 68000 had no floating-point processor, so the floating-point times are several times slower than integer (but much faster than the "no FPP" times of the previous smaller processors). Operations upon float are just enough slower to be worth a column of their own.

Multiply, divide, and remainder are again slower than other integer operations. On this processor, unsigned divides are somewhat faster. Shifts are roughly equal in speed to other integer operations.

Timing results on VAX 11/780 with UNIX System V compiler:

```
time.vax:
    Execution times for operators
    VAX 11/780 UNIX System V
    With floating-point hardware
```

Operation	register (1)	long (2)	short (3)	double (4)
"average"	1.30	1.85	2.46	7.59
s.m		0.52	0.79	
p->m	0.43	0.90	1.20	
a[k]	1.04	1.93	2.15	
(double)k	1.43	1.76	2.64	0.00
(long)k	0.0	0.020	0.63	4.93
(int)k	0.0	0.43	1.02	4.95
(char)k	3.00	0.65	1.07	4.73
&k		0.43	0.68	0.68
~k	0.43	1.07	1.46	
++k	0.43	1.12	2.35	11.7
k++	0.43	1.72	1.87	
!k	1.45	1.97	2.00	3.97
-k	0.43	1.12	1.71	2.07
j * k	6.18	7.02	9.05	19.0
j / k	9.67	10.5	12.1	44.3
j % k	12.1	13.2	14.8	
j + k	0.63	1.06	3.05	10.9
j - k	0.43	1.14	2.78	11.6
j << k	1.86	2.48	3.45	
j >> k	2.07	3.08	4.07	
j <= k	1.86	2.90	2.83	7.18
j != k	1.66	2.07	2.17	7.55
j && k	2.99	3.41	3.55	5.55
j || k	2.99	3.41	3.55	5.55
j & k	1.04	2.48	3.22	
j | k	0.68	1.12	2.87	
j ^ k	0.49	1.06	2.83	
i ? j : k	2.27	3.10	3.95	5.02
j = k	0.47	1.24	0.84	3.62

```
Times are in microseconds (+30%)

(1) register int (2) long, unsigned long, int, unsigned int
(3) short, unsigned short, char, unsigned char (4) double, float

Note:  unsigned: divide is 200% slower
       unsigned: multiply is 50% slower
```

On the VAX, short integers are somewhat slower than long (i.e., int). The use of register is, again, good for about a one-third speed improvement, on the average. Floating-point execution is pleasingly brisk. The distribution of times is rather flat: the fastest and slowest times are within a factor of ten.

2.5 Applying the Timing Results

Having presented all these timing figures, we should now discuss their applicability to your environment.

The timing suite which generated these figures made sure that at least 100 clock ticks, above the time required for the harness, were obtained for each sample. When the timings were run on an idle system, we verified experimentally that this gave repeatable timings accurate to one percent. The tables, however, group "similar" combinations of type and storage class, and within each category there were variations as large as 30%, so we conservatively describe them as accurate to plus or minus 30%.

On systems with special hardware features (e.g., larger VAXs) you may see a 10% (or greater) variability in your executions due to the hit rate in the cache. A cache is a special high speed memory which allows machine instructions to be executed with less delay than is associated with accessing "regular" memory.

The hit rate is affected by many factors including the system loading at the time of the test and the size of the loop which may be executing when the timing is done.

Our timing studies all tested the execution of fairly tight loops, whose referenced variables were likely to remain in the cache. Thus, the timings may be significantly faster than would be obtained in a normal program.

Other factors include the type and speed of memory in which the program is running. On some systems, there can be a considerable difference between the access time of the memory which is on the main processor board and any additional memory boards which are added in the expansion slots.

In systems where the access to the memory is shared between the processor and another piece of hardware (e.g., DMA or graphics hardware) it is possible to have considerable variability in the running time due to a phenomenon known as cycle stealing. Cycle stealing refers to the fact that a block of memory can only be accessed by a single processor or device at any given time. When a processor goes to memory to fetch an instruction or operand it may have to wait if another processor or device is accessing the memory at the same time. This other processor or device is "stealing" memory access cycles from the main processor. This causes the main processor to run more slowly than it would if it had immediate access to the memory. In some cases cycle stealing is regular and can be discounted since it will always occur (e.g., regular screen refreshing) however, others (e.g., DMA access of memory) are intermittent and, in general, non-repeatable.

The 68000 timings present special problems of interpretation. The 68000 is used in a wide variety of board configurations, with varying clock rates and varying numbers of memory wait states. Our processor ran at 10MHz with one wait state; if your processor has one wait state, you can simply multiply our results by the ratio of clock rates. For example, if your processor runs at 8 MHZ with one wait state, your times will be 20% larger than ours. If your processor has a different number of wait states, see the appendix for suggestions on comparing the timing results [2-4].

2.6 Control Structures

A C program consists of more than just operators, of course. The control structures also take time to execute, so we will consider their timings next. We need to address the if, for, while. do, and switch statements along with the overhead involved in function calls.

The if statement

Due to the approach we have taken in timing the relational operators there is no additional timing overhead which needs to be added when an if statement is encountered. The code which handles the test and jumping to the appropriate branch of the if was measured (in only a slightly different form) when we measured the assignment of a result of a relational expression to a variable. We can see this more clearly if we look at the way code must be generated for a statement like

    i = j < k;

where i, j, and k are all integer variables.

First the code to load and compare j and k must be generated. At this point code must be generated which will assign a 1 to i if the result of the comparison is true and assign a 0 to i if the result of the comparison is false. The branching required to accomplish this is essentially the same as the branching required to jump to the appropriate branch of an if statement after a comparison.

The only place where we need to be careful is in statements like

```
if (is_empty)
```

In this statement we must remember that there is an *implicit* comparison against 0. It is as if the compiler converted the above statement into

```
if (is_empty != 0)
```

and thereby introduced a comparison operator.

It is also worth noting that most compilers handle the logical NOT (!) operator by simply reversing the sense of the comparison, rather than actually doing a specific NOT operation on the result. This means that

```
if (is_empty)
```

and

```
if (!is_empty)
```

will typically generate the same amount of executable code.

In summary, the cost of the if statement can be reasonably estimated to be the cost, as we have already measured it, of the relational expression contained in the condition.

Loops

The estimation of the looping statements of C (for, while, and do) can be handled in the same way that the if statement was handled. A good rough estimate of the time required for a for statement is simply the sum of the costs of the initialization, completion test, and increment. The time required for while and do statement can reasonably be estimated to be the time required for the test which follows the while in each case. As was discussed in the previous section, this is true because of the way the relational operators were measured for our earlier tables.

The switch statement

The switch statement is somewhat more complicated than the previous statements. We are aware of at least three ways of implementing the switch. The first is as a series of nested if statements. This has the advantage of being simple and fast, for switch statements with a small number of cases.

The second approach is to use a "jump table." A jump table has an entry for each possible value between the lowest and highest values specified in the case labels. Each entry contains the address of the code which is to be executed when the associated switch value is handled by the case. The jump table is augmented by tests to direct the control flow around the switch, or to the default case, if the switch value is not in the range handled by the jump table. The actual switch value is used to calculate an index into the jump table. The program continues execution at the address selected from the table. This approach has the advantage of being very compact for switches which have a large number of contiguous or almost contiguous cases. It also has the nice feature that the first and last cases are accessed equally fast. It has the disadvantage that for widely separated cases a very large jump table is generated.

The third approach is a table of value-address pairs. This table is walked by a simple piece of code which compares the switch value with the value part of the table. If a match is found then the execution continues at the associated address.

Most compilers do not limit themselves to a single approach. Depending on the particular switch, many compilers will select between the first and second alternatives above. The third alternative may also be an option, but this is less frequently seen. The compiler may do calculations to determine which one is more efficient, so that it can generate the appropriate code. The specific point where it becomes more advantageous to use one approach over another varies from machine to machine and from implementation to implementation.

If multiple techniques are used by a compiler they can generally be broken into two cases, the few/sparse case (e.g., case labels 1, 10, and 100) and the many/dense case (e.g., case labels 1 through 100 with no omissions). If the "nested if" or "value and address" pairs approaches are going to be used, they will be used in the few/sparse case. This is because of the excessive overhead in a jump table for individual entries for each possible value between the high and low extremes of the case labels in the few/sparse case.

When the few/sparse case is handled with either the "nested if" or "value and address" pair approaches, then the time required for the switch statement is made up of a fixed overhead plus additional time for each case which must be handled. The following tables show the numbers for our four comparison compilers.

switch: few/sparse

	8088/PC Lattice	PDP-11/23 WSL	MC68000 V/68	VAX-11/780 UNIX V
fixed overhead (usec)	8.3	25.	13.9	6.4
per-case time (usec)	4.5 (1)	12.2 (1)	3.0	1.4

(1) last case is reached fastest,
    first case is reached slowest

If a compiler offers the jump table for a switch statement, then it will used in the many/dense case. Here the jump table is generally more compact and faster than either of the other two methods. As was noted previously, the jump table approach has the feature that all items are accessed equally fast. We therefore only need to determine how long it takes to access any item in the case and we can use this time for all many/dense case switches. The following times show the results of the time required to access any case in the many/dense case.

switch: many/dense

	8088/PC Lattice	PDP-11/23 WSL	MC68000 V/68	VAX-11/780 UNIX V
fixed overhead (usec)	34.6	25.	15.6	7.
per-case time (usec)	0.	12.2 (1)	0.	0.

(1) last case is reached fastest,
    first case is reached slowest

It is up to the programmer to classify a switch as being few/sparse or many/dense. Many compilers use a simple algorithm to determine the point where the compiler will move from using the few/sparse case to the many/dense case. Some simple experimenting with the amount of time it takes to access the first case versus the amount of time it takes to access the last case in the switch can be done to help determine which category a particular switch belongs in.

2.7 Function Calls and Returns

The time required for function calls is made up of a fixed overhead (for the call and return) plus an additional increment for each argument which is passed [2-5]. The following table shows the time required for a function call and return in the evaluated systems. The first time shown was produced by calling a function with one register (local) variable, while the second time was produced by calling a function with no local variables. Neither function had any arguments; the differences in times for the two cases are due to different "prolog" function-entry sequences.

```
function call/return
                    8088/PC   PDP-11/23    MC68000  VAX-11/780
                    Lattice         WSL       V/68      UNIX V

function call (usec)   36.0        64.4       14.1        19.4
call (no registers)    19.0        26.2       11.9        16.3

per-arg time (usec)     5.          9.         4.          1.
```

The "per-arg" time is an average based upon tests with zero, one, two, and three arguments; the relationship is not exactly linear, but the differences are not significant enough to distinguish.

2.8 Libraries

In many cases, the dominant factor in a timing estimate will be the execution time of library functions in the inner loops, rather than the times for individual operators in the application program. We therefore undertook to time some representative functions from the libraries.

In many cases, library function timings depend upon many different variables. In the interests of brevity, we have selected only a small number of illustrations. Use the figures for rough estimation. Wherever a particular function call is critical to an algorithm, it is easy enough to make a specific test harness for that case.

Timings for the math library:

```
mathtime.tbl:
```

	8088/PC Lattice (FPP)	8088/PC Lattice (no FPP)	PDP-11/23 WSL (FPP)	PDP-11/23 WSL (no FPP)	MC68000 V/68 (no FPP)	VAX-11/780 UNIX V (FPP)
atan(x)	.433	47.1	1.96	25.0	6.4	.531
cos(x)	.727	49.0	3.12	63.3	6.9	.611
exp(x)	.658	36.6	3.15	63.8	6.2	.481
log(x)	.271	9.15	3.74	88.1	2.52	.218
log10(x)	.281	12.3	4.07	97.8	2.94	.271
pow(x, y)	.647	43.9	7.40	169.	9.29	.901
sin(x)	.755	40.1	3.35	71.8	4.37	.513
sqrt(x)	.277	21.8	2.94	66.8	4.85	.448

```
times are in milliseconds
```

Once again, the difference between FPP and non-FPP is very striking, for systems that have both possibilities. It is important to note that these times are in milliseconds, not microseconds. Thus, with no FPP, a math function call is equivalent to a thousand C operations (to an order of magnitude). With an FPP, the equivalence is more like one hundred operations.

The execution speeds on the (FPP-assisted) 8088 are due to the micro-coding of the math functions into the 8087 chip itself.

The timings of math functions are likely to be very data-dependent. We used values of .5 for all arguments.

Timings for the character-test library:

```
ctypetime.tbl:
```

	8088/PC Lattice	PDP-11/23 WSL	MC68000 V/68	VAX-11/780 UNIX V
isalnum(c)	12.9	18.	8.5	3.0
isalpha(c)	12.9	18.	8.5	3.1
isascii(c)	8.8	17.	5.4	2.6
iscntrl(c)	12.9	18.	8.5	3.5
isdigit(c)	12.9	18.	8.5	3.5
islower(c)	12.8	18.	8.5	3.5
isprint(c)	12.8	18.	8.5	3.5
ispunct(c)	12.9	18.	8.7	3.5
isspace(c)	12.8	18.	8.7	3.5
isupper(c)	12.9	18.	8.5	3.5
tolower(c)	29.2	68.	27.2	23.1
toupper(c)	29.2	68.	27.8	23.1

The character-test functions are typically implemented as macros, and their timings are indeed faster than function-call operations in each environment. The character-conversion functions (tolower and toupper) take longer because they have more work to do.

Timings for the string functions:

strtime.tbl:

	8088/PC Lattice	PDP-11/23 WSL	MC68000 V/68	VAX-11/780 UNIX V
strcat-0 chars	163.	124.	23.0	49.3
strcat-per char	3.7	8.1	2.9	.70
strchr-0 chars	110.	86.	16.6	73.6
strchr-per char	4.4	3.2	4.3	.33
strcmp-0 chars	67.2	67.	24.2	34.1
strcmp-per char	5.3	4.0	5.4	.70
strcpy-0 chars	84.7	118.	20.0	40.0
strcpy-per char	3.7	8.0	2.9	.68
strlen-0 chars	62.8	88.	14.2	23.8
strlen-per char	3.6	1.0	2.3	.38
strncat-0 chars	187.	158.	33.5	54.5
strncat-per char	54.	46.	2.9	.70
strncmp-0 chars	107.	74.	34.0	40.5
strncmp-per char	78.	40.	4.4	.69
strncpy-0 chars	111.	152.	33.9	54.3
strncpy-per char	57.	36.	2.9	.70
strcat-100 chars	3850.	936.	312.	119.
strchr-100 chars	4470.	3260.	449.	107.
strcmp-100 chars	5360.	4110.	565.	104.
strcpy-100 chars	3780.	924.	307.	108.
strlen-100 chars	3120.	1100.	249.	62.0
strncat-100 chars	5610.	4810.	324.	124.
strncmp-100 chars	7950.	4110.	470.	109.
strncpy-100 chars	5880.	3770.	320.	124.

We timed the string functions with two cases each, one which processed zero characters (except for the nul terminator where appropriate) and one which processed 100 characters. Simple linear interpolation gives a "per-character" time for each function, as shown. The top part of the table shows the "zero" and "per-character" times, with the raw data for the '100-character" timing given below.

To an order of magnitude, we could conclude that each character costs a small number of microseconds of processor time.

Timings for I/O functions:

stdiotime.tbl:

	8088/PC Lattice	PDP-11/23 WSL	MC68000 V/68	VAX-11/780 UNIX V
fopen, fclose	2170.	62.0	16.2	8.23
fgetc	.214	.279	.036	.028
fgets-100 chars	10.6	4.49	.507	.24
fprintf-%d	9.86	3.07	1.17	.316
fprintf-%d %d	24.0	5.67	2.26	.546
fputc	.573	.218	.039	.027
fputs-100 chars	43.4	7.04	.677	.236
fread-100 chars	29.7	48.3	.809	.343
fread-BUFSIZ chars	141.0	75.8	6.78	2.61
fscanf-1 int	1.88	2.81	.622	.333
fscanf-2 ints	4.05	5.29	1.18	.618
fseek, fgetc	143.0	33.2	4.96	1.73
fwrite-100 chars	47.6	9.21	.614	.194
fwrite-BUFSIZ chars	282.0	3.39	4.54	.593
sprintf-1 int	7.78	2.57	.997	.266
sprintf-2 ints	15.5	4.79	1.9	.45
sscanf-1 int	1.82	4.62	2.09	.848
sscanf-2 ints	3.72	9.11	2.98	1.26

times are in milliseconds

fdtime.tbl:

	8088/PC Lattice	PDP-11/23 WSL	MC68000 V/68	VAX-11/780 UNIX V
open, close	370.	41.7	14.7	7.1
read-BUFSIZ chars	110.	16.2	3.48	1.98
lseek, read-BUFSIZ	179.	18.3	5.61	2.85
write-BUFSIZ chars	686.	2.19	1.34	.53

times are in milliseconds

In the I/O libraries we see most dramatically the capacity differences between environments. In some cases, there is almost a 100:1 ratio between the largest and smallest times. Note: all times are in milliseconds, not microseconds.

The timings for fopen and open are highly dependent upon the directory size. The directories in which these tests were run were quite large, with 100 to 150 entries. On the two small systems we reran timings for the "open" functions in small directories with only four or five entries. The difference is striking:

	8088/PC Lattice	PDP-11/23 WSL
Large directory:		
fopen, fclose	2170.	62.0
open, close	370.	41.7
Small directory:		
fopen, fclose	66.8	28.5
open, close	263.	14.2

One final observation: on non-UNIX systems (such as MS-DOS), there is a distinction between text and binary files. In the Lattice 2.15 (8088) environment, the default file type is "text," which requires character-by-character translation. The expected throughput of fread/fwrite and read/write would be much greater if "binary" mode is specified. (See Plum [1985] regarding "binary" I/O.)

2.9 Summary

As we saw in Chapter 1, it can be useful to characterize each machine by an "average C operator." As a very rough approximation, we could say that the small systems — 8088 and PDP-11/23 — are "10 microsecond" machines. The 68000 (in this configuration) is a "5 microsecond" machine, and the VAX 11/780 is a "2 microsecond" machine. In each environment, those operations that are not supported by hardware — 32-bit or FPP — take so much longer that they will probably dominate our timing estimate. In other words, on a machine like PDP-11/23, in an algorithm involving long multiplies, we can get rough estimates just by counting the multiplies.

We can summarize the rest of our findings with "rules of thumb" based on these very rough "average operator" equivalents. These rules are intended only to give you an intuitive feel for the time requirements of various parts of a C program.

A switch is a few (three or so) times more expensive than an average operation. A function call takes three to six times as long as an average operation, with a small extra overhead per argument.

Calling a math function costs (very roughly) a hundred operations if FPP support is available, and a thousand operations without FPP. The character-type tests are quick, averaging only one or two operators. The string functions average less than one operator per character moved or examined. The I/O functions vary widely in timing. The fgetc, getchar, fputc, and putchar calls are fastest: less than 10 operators, on the average. The other functions take on the order of 100 operators, and "text-mode" I/O may be slower, on non-UNIX systems.

Now that you have an intuitive feel for the time requirements of C programs, we will look next at general efficiency techniques — those techniques which are not just specific to C.

CHAPTER 3: GENERAL EFFICIENCY TECHNIQUES

In this chapter we will discuss the efficiency techniques that are applicable to programming projects in general, whether the target language is C or not. First we will discuss guidelines for estimating, and then we will cover common techniques for improving time efficiency.

3.1 Advance Estimates of Time

We will now address the estimation of the size and speed of our program. How often do we care, early in an project, how big and fast the resulting program will be? In a professional software development environment, surprisingly often.

When a software developer is given a specification for a new product, it almost always includes some performance requirements (e.g., the C compiler will compile at least 4000 lines a minute) and some size and hardware constraints (e.g., it must run in 64K on an IBM PC). The software developer should determine whether it is possible to meet these requirements (some of which may be mutually exclusive from an engineering perspective).

It has been our experience that software developers frequently accept these requirements as targets without any real confidence that they will be met. Software developers typically figure that if they design the product as well as they can that the product will be acceptably fast and small. This often leads to serious problems when, near the very end of a project, it is "discovered" that the program is twice as big as was specified and half as fast.

Tony Hoare [1980] tells the story of a compiler development where the initial development resulted in a compiler which ran at 4 lines a minute. They went back and doubled the speed ... up to 8 lines a minute ... and then to 16 but this was significantly more difficult and they still realized that they were many more doublings away from having an acceptable product. Eventually the project was scrapped (with a great loss in time and money).

Clearly, techniques must be developed to determine early in the development cycle whether the program, as designed, will meet the time and space requirements of the application. These will help eliminate the enormous waste of effort that occurs when a major project is scrapped because the resulting product is unacceptably slow or big.

3.2 What About "First, Make It Right"?

Worrying about how big or fast a piece of code will be before it is written seems to be opposed to the approach, espoused earlier in this book, of "Make it right before you make it fast."

A simplistic interpretation of "Make it right before you make it fast" would be to totally ignore time and space efficiency considerations until after the program has been coded and is working.

The major problem with this approach is that if the fundamental design is inadequate then no amount of post-development fix up will make the program fast (small) enough to be workable. The only viable alternative may be to scrap the entire effort, chalk it up to experience, and start over by looking for an algorithm or approach which may meet the specifications.

There are even times when the algorithm is as efficient as is possible and the only possible solution for acceptable performance is a faster processor. When designing a complete hardware and software system it may be possible to change processors early in the design process, but changes late in the development become prohibitively expensive because of the investment in processor-specific hardware and software design and development. This makes an early determination of problems of paramount importance.

Even in the case where the software can be salvaged by changes to a few key algorithms and data structures the cost can be higher than is first expected. While modular programming limits the effects of algorithm changes to a single (or at most, a few) modules, required changes to key global data structures can cause changes to code which is not directly part of the performance or space bottleneck.

The whole process of making changes when limited local changes are not sufficient can be a very costly and time consuming process (and since time to market is often the difference between success and failure, can mean the project's overall success or failure).

3.3 A Qualified "Make It Right" Rule

Part of developing a program which is "right" is developing one which meets the time and space constraints imposed by the application. It is, therefore, important to consider the time and space requirements as important as any other functional requirement in a program specification, particularly during the design phase of a program.

This early emphasis on efficiency issues is in no way intended to be a license to ignore all the valid requirements of code readability and maintainability under the guise of squeezing bytes just to make sure the program will fit. It is a requirement on the software designer to apply appropriate estimation techniques so that he has confidence that the design will meet the time and space requirements. If there are critical areas or functions, these can be highlighted so the programmer can be aware that research or special care may be appropriate for the coding of these functions and their associated data structures.

Emphasis on size and speed considerations during the design phase of a program is not intended to encourage a development where trade-offs between clear simple code and optimized less clear code always falls towards the optimized less clear code. In fact, by doing estimations of the key pieces of code, it may become obvious that the algorithm is well within the constraints and that simplicity, readability, and maintainability should remain the foremost considerations for the entire program.

3.4 When and How To Estimate

Since estimation techniques are an important tool for the software designer, the question now is and when and how do we do the appropriate estimations.

There are three issues which must be addressed. First, we must know when to spend the time and effort to estimate. Second, we must determine what we should estimate. Third, we must know how to estimate.

Estimation is usually not warranted in small to medium scale programs where there are no significant time or space constraints. Frequently formal estimation is not required when similar efforts have been done previously, and the resulting programs worked within the general time and space constraints for this application. "Experience" is probably the most important informal estimating tool currently used.

Applications where the techniques and algorithms are well researched and tested, and the results when given specific types of inputs are understood (e.g., searching and sorting), may not require estimation work before actually implementing a design.

Spending time doing estimations is often not warranted when prototypes of a software system are being developed. Prototypes usually deal with the feasibility and functionality of a software system rather than concentrating on efficiency issues.

Estimation can be very useful in small projects which have severe time or space constraints. It is particularly important when it is difficult to test all of the extreme conditions that may occur. A real-time controller may be one such case. A certain amount of processing frequently has to be done in a specific window of time, or additional information may be lost. The code simply must complete in that time window. Knowing how long a piece of code will take is an important aspect of knowing whether it is "right." Estimation is doubly important in such applications because empirical measurements are often difficult and tricky.

Estimation probably pays the biggest dividends when it is done during the design stages of a large software project. These projects, due to their size and complexity, are very susceptible to serious size and space problems.

As was noted above, the easiest way to get this estimate is to find someone who has done this type of program before and find out how they did it and how big and fast the resulting program was.

Unfortunately, in the real world, such experts seldom seem to be available when you need them. Even if an expert is available you may be doing something which has not been done before (at least not in this particular environment). In this case, previous experience is valuable, but not necessarily sufficient to supply an accurate estimate.

When we decide that it is appropriate to do an estimation, the question becomes "what to estimate." When a program or function is small, it is practical to do an estimation on the complete program. This is how a real-time controller might be addressed. When dealing with large software systems it is impractical to do time and space estimations on the entire system. Since, by definition, we are working with a large body of code we need to be selective about what pieces to estimate. Only the *key* pieces should be addressed. However, software developers are notoriously bad at guessing where the bottlenecks are going to occur in a piece of code. We need to have some guidelines on what to look for.

While recognizing that each project presents unique challenges, we can still suggest three general guidelines. First, do detailed estimations for all components which are known in advance to be time-critical: interrupt latencies, interactive response limits, time constraints in the controlled process, etc. Second, attend to all the inner loops of the program: even a rough estimate of each loop's execution time can give us advance warning of potential bottlenecks. Third, make a list of the functions and operations which are disproportionately slow on the target machine: this might include long arithmetic, or floating arithmetic, or I/O functions. Then examine the design or program for instances in which these slow operations are performed in time-critical contexts.

Now we consider "how to estimate." Once we have determined what we need to estimate, we now need to know how to estimate how long this code will take to execute or how much space it will require.

The measurement background which we have established in the previous chapter allows us to tackle this part of the job.

In many cases the simplest way to get an estimate is to code the key section of an algorithm and do some timings on the resulting code. This can be done using the timing tools which were used to generate our timings in Chapter 2 (and are discussed in more detail in the appendix).

However, it is not always possible or convenient to code and time a section of code. It may be very difficult to simulate the inputs for the section of code, (e.g., complex data structures may have to be built, initialized and updated). It may be difficult to simulate, in real time, the environment (e.g., interrupt conditions) which will be present when the code will be executing.

The target machine where the code is going to run may not support convenient code timings.

When timings are not practical, then the estimates have to be done manually. The fundamental approach is to simply add up the time and/or space required by the statements and operators in the code, as we did in Chapter 1.

When estimating, it is important to remember that the compiler may do optimizations which will invalidate a simple addition of the times. That is, the program may outperform the estimate, which is usually good news. In Section 3.8, we will discuss some optimizations that C compilers may make.

3.5 Additional Benefits from Estimation

One important aspect of estimation is that it draws our attention to some of the key factors which have direct bearing on the efficiency of the code. The process of actually adding in the additional time or space for each statement and operator (e.g., a division of a `double` variable) makes us come to understand exactly what the bottlenecks and problem areas are.

By using the estimation techniques we can quickly determine the effects of placing different variables into the register. We can use our estimation techniques as a way of saying "what if." It becomes clear that it is not only frequency of use but also the type of use which determines the best variables to place into registers.

3.6 Compiler Options

When you decide, after measuring or estimating, that you must improve the time efficiency of a program you must look for ways to bring about this improvement.

The first place to look, on many systems, is your compiler. Some compilers offer an optimizer pass which can be invoked by special options on the compiler command line. For example, in UNIX environments a C compiler optimization pass is invoked by using the -O option:

```
cc -O file.c
```

Optimizers, if they are available, have widely varying degrees of effectiveness. The optimizers that we are familiar with typically produce space and time savings of between 5 and 15 percent over the unoptimized code. This improvement can be obtained without any recoding on the programmer's part and therefore offers an attractive alternative for programs that are *almost* fast or small enough. One caution: separate optimization passes have, in some cases, contained bugs which were not present in the compiler itself.

Of the four environments which we are using for comparisons in this book, the Lattice and Whitesmiths compilers do not have separate optimization passes. The 68000 V/68 and VAX UNIX System V compilers offer separate optimization passes via the -O option.

The lack of an optimization pass is not necessarily a sign of less efficient code generation. Many of the compiler optimizations which we will be discussing in a later section are included in the default processing of the compilers. This means that the Lattice and Whitesmiths compilers (and other compilers which do not have independent optimization passes) produce the best code the compiler can generate on every run. In contrast, the UNIX compilers can be directed to spend extra time in compilation if optimization is required. Less efficient code is generated, with correspondingly shorter compilation times, when efficiency is not an issue.

3.7 Design and Coding Techniques

If the compiler optimization pass does not improve the efficiency of the program enough, then the next step is to review the algorithm and data structures, in an attempt to find places where they can be improved. If the problem is not being addressed for the first time, then it is possible that faster algorithms (possibly due to improved data structures) for the specific problem or a very similar one are available in the literature. Frequently, a day or two of research in books on the topic being addressed or into the related technical journals can save weeks of trial-and-error work.

If a better algorithm or data structure for the specific problem is not available, then the next step is to consider one of the many general language-independent optimizations which can be used to improve the time efficiency of the program. Although these general optimization techniques are not the primary focus of this book, we will give the following list, with a brief discussion, as a check-list of ideas which may apply to your particular algorithm or problem.

Most of the following optimizations can be applied to any part of a program. However, in most programs, most of the CPU time is taken by small portions of the code, usually inner loops — the so-called "hot spots." It is therefore usually worthwhile to concentrate on the loops which are executed frequently to see if improvements can be made there. The importance of concentrating on heavily executed sections of code is clearer when we consider that doubling the speed of a section of code which accounts for 50% of the total execution time will speed up the overall program 25% while doubling the speed of a section of code which only accounts for 2% of the total execution time will only speed up the overall program 1%. It frequently requires the same effort independent of the the resulting payoff.

Here, then, is a list of design and coding techniques for improving CPU-time efficiency, sometimes at the expense of space utilization.

Move code out of loops

One key improvement is to move code out of loops, particularly nested loops. Look for operations which give the same result each time through the loop. These operations can be moved out of the loop and executed only once. Watch for expressions which do not depend on the loop index.

Unroll loops

Loop unrolling is the process of duplicating (possibly many times) the code from the body of a loop to reduce the loop overhead costs, by reducing the number of times that the completion test in the loop is executed. The extreme case is to eliminate the loop completely and to do the work as straight line code. Complete loop unrolling also eliminates the processing related to updating the loop index variable. It may also have the side benefit of causing variable array subscripts to be replaced by constant subscripts which are almost always faster.

Consider this loop which reverses the byte-ordering of a small array of chars:

```
for (i = 0; i < 8; i += 2)
    SWAP(buf[i], buf[i+1], tempc);
```

Written as straight-line code, it looks like this:

```
SWAP(buf[0], buf[1], tempc);
SWAP(buf[2], buf[3], tempc);
SWAP(buf[4], buf[5], tempc);
SWAP(buf[6], buf[7], tempc);
```

Merge loops

Merging loops (also called loop fusion) is the process of combining two or more loops into one so that the cost of the loop overhead is paid only once. The most frequent opportunities for loop fusion arise during initialization processing where two arrays of the same size are initialized with two consecutive loops rather than a single loop:

```
for (i = 0; i < N; ++i)     becomes     for (i = 0; i < N; ++i)
    a[i] = f1(i);                        {
for (i = 0; i < N; ++i)                      a[i] = f1(i);
    b[i] = f2(i);                            b[i] = f2(i);
                                        }
```

Reorder tests

When a series of logical tests are to be performed, and when one of them is significantly faster and capable of determining the result, then the faster test should be done first.

The C language is well-suited for this type of optimization because the logical AND (&&) and logical OR (||) operations are short-circuited. This means that evaluation of each of the operands is only done until the truth or falsity of the expression is determined. For the AND, this means that the second operand will not be evaluated if the first operand is false (because the result is guaranteed to be false). Similarly, the second operand of the OR is never evaluated if the first operand is true.

You can use this information to your advantage by ordering your tests so that the tests which are more likely to be true occur first in logical OR expressions and last in logical AND expressions. This approach will reduce the average amount of time spent in the evaluation of these expressions.

Sometimes it will be worth introducing an extra test, if it is fast and it will almost always determine the result. For example, in the Plum Hall local.h header is the macro STREQ ("string equal"):

```
#define STREQ(s1, s2) (strcmp(s1, s2) == 0)
```

Usually, different strings differ in their very first character, so we could revise STREQ to take more code space and less CPU time:

```
#define STREQ(s1, s2) (*(s1) == *(s2) && strcmp(s1, s2) == 0)
```

Simplify Computations

Simple, elegant solutions are frequently the key to reducing excessive computation time. For example, when dealing with strings where frequent manipulations are being done, it is often advantageous to save each distinct string in a table and then use a table index or a pointer into the table to represent the string in future operations. The table index (or pointer) is known as a *token*, and the process of tabulation is known as *tokenizing*. This allows a string to be assigned to a new variable by copying only the token rather than the whole string of characters. It also allows string equality comparisons to be done by comparing indices rather than comparing each of the characters in the respective strings. This technique is used in every modern compiler to speed and simply processing of program identifiers.

On a lower level you want to replace expensive operations by simpler, less expensive operations.

For example, if a value is generated by multiplying a loop index by a constant then the value can also be obtained by using an addition in place of the multiply. The multiply operation is replaced by an assignment and an addition of the constant to a variable which holds a cumulative result. For example,

```
for (i = 1; i <= 100; i++)
    {
    j[i]= i * 10;
    }
```

can be replaced by the faster

```
for (i = 1, t = 0; i <= 100; i++)
    {
    j[i] = (t += 10);
    }
```

Depending on the usage, subscripted references may be replaced by pointer references which frequently require fewer calculations. See the discussion in section 4.6 (Subscripts and Pointers) for more details.

An opportunity to eliminate a computation completely occurs when dealing with array subscripts which are always value-1. This is often seen because of the zero-origin array subscripting in C. The additional subtraction in each subscript calculation can frequently be eliminated by allocating an extra row (or column) in the array and then using rows 1 through n rather than rows 0 through n-1 for the data. This may leave the 0 row unused, but this trade frequently simplifies the subscript calculations, resulting in a faster program. The resulting program is also more readable and less likely to contain off-by-one errors.

Care must be taken not to go overboard in the area of simplifying expressions. Many compilers handle many of the simple optimizations, such as replacing multiplication by powers of 2 with left shifts. This will be discussed in more detail in the next section.

In general, if the compiler will do an optimization for you, then readability and maintainability are better served if you leave the computation in its clearest, most straightforward form.

Reduce repetitive computations

When a computation appears multiple times in a piece of code, consider doing the computation once and saving the result in a temporary location. The temporary variable is then referenced in each place where the computation originally occurred.

```
i = j * k + 9;        becomes       i = j * k + 9;
k = m + j * k + 9;                  k = i + m;
```

This process, called *common subexpression elimination*, is done automatically in some compilers, as discussed in the next section.

Precomputed values

Some functions have a limited set of input values which they will receive during the execution of a program. If these input values can be completely specified, it is possible to use a table of precomputed values to replace the action of the function.

This approach is of limited value if the number of possible inputs is large. (A table of all integer values would strain the memory on most systems.) However, a small range of values allows a reasonable tradeoff to be made between the time savings of not calculating the result and the space required to save all of the results.

In the example in our introductory chapter, we went through several versions of the bitcnt function to determine the number of bits set in a byte. The bitcnt function can use a simple array, indexed by the byte value, which tells the number of bits set in that byte. We can use the initialization facilities of C to create this table and to avoid any execution-time calculations from being done. The following example shows how this might be done:

```
bitcnt(#5):
    /* bitcnt - return the bit sum of a byte argument
     * version 5
     */
    #define BYTEMASK 0xFF
    char bitsum[256] =
        {
        0, 1, 1, 2, 1, 2, 2, 3,
        /* ... */
        };
    int bitcnt(c)
        char c;
        {
        return (bitsum[c & BYTEMASK]);
        }
```

The improvement from this approach is summarized in this table:

	8088/PC Lattice	PDP-11/23 WSL	MC68000 UNIX V	VAX-11/780 UNIX V
bitcnt V5 (actual)	58.3	50.1	26.7	20.6
improvement over V1	86%	89%	86%	78%

Note that it is usually worthwhile to develop a program to generate a large initializer like this one, rather than trying to create it by hand.

Exploit common cases

It frequently occurs that, over the total range of possible cases which a function or program must handle, a few are far more common. The average performance of a function can frequently be improved by some fast special-case processing for the common cases. This may slow down the general case, but this extra cost is only paid when the common case is not being handled. See Section 4.2 (Selecting Data Types for Speed) for an example of special case processing.

Cacheing

A frequently useful form of special casing is cacheing. In cacheing you save the result or data from the current processing. This is done with the expectation that you will be able to generate the result more quickly the *next* time the function is called, because the value or data is available.

For example, if a function is frequently called with the same argument, then the majority of the work can be avoided by saving the last result returned and simply returning the previously calculated value if the function argument (and any key global variables) contain the same values as on the previous call.

Cacheing is also very useful when information must be read from a file to complete the processing of a function. If data must be read in from disk storage it is frequently worth saving the data (along with where it came from) so that the I/O does not have to be repeated if the same data is required the next time the function is called. A list of data items may be kept if a small set of data items is being referenced.

Note that cacheing does not pay off if the next function call is not likely to require the same information to complete the function's processing. The overhead of checking to see whether the information is already in memory simply slows down the average time for the function with only occasional benefits.

Remember that static or global variables must be used to save the values between function invocations since auto variables are recreated on each function invocation.

Augment the data structures

We can generalize the idea of cacheing, which saves only the most "recent" value(s) and save all of the values which have been calculated. If considerable time is being spent recalculating values, it may be faster to augment or build a data structure to save the values the first time they are calculated so that they only need to be computed once. This approach usually results in a faster, larger program (i.e., trades space for time).

Quickly eliminate alternatives

When large amounts of information must be searched it is advantageous to limit the search to only a small portion of the total information as quickly as possible. This is the basic idea behind the use of binary trees for searching (Plum [1985]); half of the remaining table of items is eliminated at each step during the search process. This is also the idea behind hashing, which takes the target item to be searched for and generates a key value which is then used to direct further searching. Only those entries which generate the same key value are searched for the desired target item.

This technique can also be used when evaluating incoming information which can be grouped into several different categories. If there are a large number of possible types in the incoming information then determining the category quickly by means of range tests can simplify and speed up the program. An example of this approach can be seen in compilers which group all keywords (e.g., if, while) at the beginning of the table of names so that a simple test on the table index of a name can be used to determine if the identifier is a keyword or a user-defined identifier.

The key idea here is to use data structures and coding techniques to convert a time-consuming task into a small manageable task as quickly as possible.

The preceding list of techniques is not a comprehensive list of all possible language-independent optimizations. The intent here is to give you a starting point. There are several excellent sources which can be referenced if further details are needed on these or other similar optimizations or improved algorithms. For more specific details, you might consult Bentley [1982] or Knuth [1973, 1981].

In the next chapter we will consider efficiency issues that are specific to C language.

CHAPTER 4: EFFICIENT CODING IN C

Up to this point we have discussed many details related to measuring how long the code related to operators and individual statements will take to execute, as well as optimizations that are common to many different languages.

In this chapter we will take our timings a step further and look into specific C language features which allow us to produce time efficient programs. We will also investigate the use of these techniques so that you understand the strengths and weaknesses of each of the techniques presented.

First, we will look at the optimizations which can be done automatically by the compiler.

4.1 Compiler Optimizations

It is useful to understand what compilers will and will not do for you. You will not generate a more efficient program if you recode a C program to manually implement an optimization which the compiler is already doing, or will do if the optimization pass is used. This recoding, however, may be costly in terms of the time to make the changes. It can have a negative impact on the readability, maintainability, and possibly even correctness (if an error is introduced by using an incorrect or unsafe "improvement") of the program.

Let us look more closely at some common compiler optimizations.

Constant Folding

One of the most common optimizations is to evaluate expressions or subexpressions which contain only constant operands during the compilation rather than generating code which will do the evaluation during the execution of the program. For example, if the statement

    j = 20 * 3;

is encountered, a compiler which does constant folding will evaluate

    20 * 3

and actually generate code as if the statement were

    j = 60;

While users do not normally write expressions such as the one just shown, it is not unusual to have constant expressions when #define's are used to create macros which serve as named constants. If the compiler folds constant expressions, then the programmer does not have to be concerned about eliminating these types of expressions when hand-optimizing the code. All four of the example compilers performed this simple form of constant-folding. Indeed, C language requires that constant-folding take place for case labels and array bounds in declarations, so most compilers are likely to do simple constant folding wherever possible.

Another place where a compiler does constant folding is where an array is referenced with a constant subscript. Here the operations involved with array references (multiplying the index times the size of each element in the array and adding this value to the starting address of the array) are done during compilation and only the address of the desired element is placed into the generated code. This was done by all four of the compilers evaluated.

Some compilers, particularly cross compilers which generate code for another machine, might only do constant folding for integer type operands. They might not fold expressions which contain floating-point constants.

Users need to be cautious in cross-compiler environments where floating constant folding is done using the host rather than the target machine's floating point arithmetic. A common error in cross compilers which use the compiler's host floating point arithmetic during constant folding is that results for the same operation will be different when evaluated by the compiler and when it is evaluated during execution. This is because floating-point arithmetic is inexact, and there may be differences between the precision of the mantissa or differences in details such as the rounding modes or the size of intermediate results. For example, a test like the one in the following code fragment may fail if a compiler does its constant folding using the host floating point arithmetic rather than the target machine's floating arithmetic.

```
double x, y;

x = 1.0;
y = 10.0;
z = x / y;
if (z >= 1.0 / 10.0)
    /* ... */
```

Assuming that only constant folding is being done, the calculation x / y will be done at execution time using the target machine floating point, and the expression 1.0 / 10.0 will be done at compilation time [4-1].

Similar considerations apply when programmers do the folding of floating point calculations by hand in an attempt to improve the efficiency of a program.

The whole area of floating-point arithmetic must be handled with care, due to differing properties on various machines. (See Hamming [1973] or Sterbenz [1974].)

In the four environments which we reviewed (none of which were cross compilers), all four compilers did constant folding for both integer and floating constant expressions. This optimization was done during the normal default processing. It did not require an optimizer pass.

Constant folding with propagation

An extension to constant folding is for the compiler to recognize when a variable has taken on a constant value and to use this information to find additional opportunities for constant folding. For example, in the previous code fragment the variables had fixed constant values (1.0 and 10.0, respectively) when the expression x / y was reached. A compiler which does constant folding with propagation will detect this kind of situation and will convert the calculation into a simple constant. In this case, the compiler which does constant folding with propagation will generate code for x / y as if it were .1 .

The only compiler evaluated which did constant folding with propagation was the Lattice C compiler.

Constant folding with rearrangement

Another approach to finding opportunities for constant folding is to use the algebraic laws of associativity and commutativity to rearrange expressions so that constants are grouped together and can be folded out. If the compiler does this type of optimization then the code for a statement like

    i = j + 7 + k + 15;

would be generated as if it were

    i = j + k + 22;

It should be noted that a C compiler is free to rearrange the terms of an expression even in the presence of parentheses, if the operators involved are all instances of the same commutative-associative operator (+, *, &, |, or ^).

The 68000 V/68 and VAX UNIX V compilers both do rearrangement of expressions to find more efficient ways of generating code. This is not done in the Lattice 2.15 and Whitesmiths 2.3 compilers.

Algebraic identities

Algebraic identities, such as the addition of 0 to a value, the multiplication of a value by 0, and the multiplication of a value by 1, can be recognized by a compiler. Simplified code, which does not actually do the computation, can then be generated.

In many ways this is similar to the constant folding previously discussed. The compiler is able to determine the value of the expression during compilation and simply inserts the result of the operation into the generated code. Consider the statement

    i = j * 1;

The compiler which recognizes the algebraic identity will generate code as if the statement were

    i = j;

This optimization may appear to be of limited value because most programmers do not write expressions like the one in our example. This kind of expression, however, can occur commonly in C code which uses macros which are replaced by constant values. In our example environments, all four optimized e * 1. Only Whitesmiths 2.3 optimized e * 0. All but Whitesmiths 2.3 optimized e + 0.

Increment/decrement instructions

Depending on the architecture and instruction set of a machine, a compiler may recognize special cases which allow the substitution of a general operation with a specialized, faster operation.

The most common occurrences of this are the "increment" and "decrement" cases. Many hardware architectures have special instructions which will increment or decrement a location by one (or some small number) more quickly than the same operation can be done using the general addition or subtraction operators.

C specifically supplies the ability to let the programmer "tell" the compiler that this special operator may be in order with the pre- and post-increment operators (++) and the pre- and post-decrement operators (--).

In the four compilers which we reviewed we found that the increment and decrement operators produced increment or decrement instructions, whenever possible.

Of the compilers evaluated, only the Whitesmiths 2.3 and Lattice 2.15 compilers recognized this special case when the expression is written out using the addition operator, for example

```
i = i + 1;
```

The fact that the compilers were inconsistent in this area leads to the recommendation that writers of efficient C programs should use the increment (++) and decrement (--) operators rather than the longer addition or subtraction form of the operation.

Multiplication and left shift

Another common optimization on ones- and twos-complement machines is that the multiplication of integer variables by powers of 2 can be replaced by left shifts. For example, a compiler which does this optimization would generate code for the statement

```
i = j * 4;
```

as if it were

```
i = j << 2;
```

This optimization was recognized and done by all of the compilers compared.

Division and right shift

In a similar manner, division of unsigned integer variables by powers of 2 can be replaced by right shifts. Note that the division of a signed integer variable cannot, in general, be replaced by a right shift.

The 68000 V/68 and Lattice 2.15 compilers apply this optimization while the others evaluated did not.

Increment/decrement with indirection

Another opportunity for optimization is found on machines which have an addressing mode or instruction which combines indirection ("dereferencing") with incrementing or decrementing. Examples of this are the PDP-11, VAX, and 68000 processors. This allows a compiler to recognize the special cases *p++ and *--p (where the pointer p is in register storage) to generate faster, more compact code. The example compilers for these three machines did, in fact, perform these optimizations.

Tests on the 8088, which does not have these special hardware addressing modes, showed no degradation in performance when the combined form *p++ was used rather than the split form of two separate statements.

These facts lead to the recommendation that the combined forms *p++ and *--p be used whenever they can accurately replace the separate operations of indirection with post-incrementing or pre-decrementing. This is a minor optimization which can still have significant impact in an inner "hot spot" loop.

Constant test elimination

Another place where the compiler can take advantage of its knowledge about the program and the guaranteed result of an operation is in the area of tests which contain only a constant. For example, assuming that CONSTVAL has been defined to have a non-zero value, in the following code segment

```
if (CONSTVAL)
    ++i;
else
    --i;
```

the variable i will always be incremented, because the test in the if will always be true. A "smart" compiler can eliminate the test and the else code, while not affecting the correct operation of the program.

All of the compilers evaluated eliminated constant tests.

Other optimizations

There are other optimizations that a compiler may make. Common ones include the improved utilization of registers, improved code selection based on information which is available once all of the code has been generated (e.g., shortening long jumps to short branches), and replacing jumps to jumps with a single jump. These optimizations are very important in the overall improvement of the time efficiency of the program; however, they are almost completely out of the control of the C programmer and therefore not of pressing interest in this book.

The previous sections have discussed a good cross section of the kind of help which can be expected from C compilers which are available today. In the next sections we will explore the optimization possibilities that are unique features of the C language, and are more directly under the programmer's control.

4.2 Selecting Data Types for Speed

The data type selected can have a significant impact on the speed of a C program. This can be seen quite dramatically in the tables of operators, presented in Chapter 2, which showed that different sizes of floating point or integers can require significantly different times when used in the same operation.

Using int instead of long

In environments where the size of int is shorter than than the size of long, calculations will typically be more time-efficient using int arithmetic rather than long arithmetic.

Obviously, you cannot change every long variable into an int variable, because the int variable does not hold the same range of values as the long. However, you can write your code so that if the current value being processed is within the range of an int variable the calculations will be done using the faster int arithmetic.

Let's look at a simple example to see how this might be done. The following function, ltoa, converts a positive long integer into a sequence of ASCII decimal digits. It accepts the long value as its first argument and stores the result in the buffer pointed to by the second argument.

```
ltoa(#1):
    /*  ltoa - convert a positive long integer into
     *  a sequence of ASCII digits (in reverse order)
     *  Version 1: all arithmetic is in  long
     */
    #include "local.h"
    void ltoa(value, buf)
        long value;
        char *buf;
        {
        while (value > 0)
            {
            *buf++ = (int)(value % 10) + '0';
            value /= 10;
            }
        *buf = '\0';
        }
```

Note that in this example that the remainder (%) and the division
(/=) are both always done using long arithmetic.

The itoa function makes use of a header named local.h. In the
Plum Hall series of books, this is the conventional name for your own
local project header of standard definitions. Besides useful macros like
SWAP, it provides defined types to assist in portability, and in *Reliable
Data Structures in C* are further suggestions on preparing for ANSI C
[Plum, 1985]. Rather than describing the full structure of local.h, we
will show here an abbreviated version which will be adequate for the
programs of this book:

```
local.h:
    /* local.h - abbreviated version for use with Efficient C */
    #ifndef LOCAL_H
    #define LOCAL_H
    #include <stdio.h>

    #define TRUE        1
    #define FALSE       0
    #define SWAP(a, b, t) ((t) = (a), (a) = (b), (b) = (t))
    #define LOOPDN(r, n)  for ((r) = (n)+1; --(r) > 0; )
    #define STREQ(s, t)   (strcmp(s, t) == 0)
    #define LONG_MAX    2147483627   /* adjust to local system */
    #define INT_MAX     32767        /* adjust to local system */
    #define CHAR_BITS   8            /* adjust to local system */

    typedef int void;         /* delete if compiler supports void keyword */
    typedef char tbool;       /* "tiny Boolean" */
    typedef short metachar;   /* either valid char value, or EOF */
    typedef char *data_ptr;   /* use ANSI "void *" if available */
    typedef unsigned size_t;  /* the type returned by  sizeof() */
    #endif
```

When int is smaller than long, we can improve the performance of this function by expanding the code to include a test to see if the value which remains to be converted is still greater than that which can be held in an int variable. (This solution trades code space for improved execution time.) When the test fails, the function uses a loop which does all of the calculations using int arithmetic. The following code shows an implementation of this approach.

```
ltoa(#2):
    /*  ltoa - convert a positive long integer into
     *  a sequence of ASCII digits (in reverse order)
     *  Version 2: uses  int  where possible
     *  Uses LONG_MAX and INT_MAX from "limits.h"
     */
    #include "local.h"
    void ltoa(value, buf)
        long value;
        char *buf;
        {
        int svalue;

    #if (LONG_MAX > INT_MAX)
        while (value > INT_MAX)
            {
            *buf++ = (int)(value % 10) + '0';
            value /= 10;
            }
    #endif
        svalue = value;
        while (svalue > 0)
            {
            *buf++ = svalue % 10 + '0';
            svalue /= 10;
            }
        *buf = '\0';
        }
```

In this example the #if brackets the code which can be omitted if the int and long variables are the same size. In this case there is no need for the two loops.

We compared the two versions, using a long argument value of (1L << 24), i.e., two to the 24-th power. The results, as expected, show the second version to be significantly faster than the first in those environments in which long is larger than int:

	8088/PC Lattice	PDP-11/23 WSL	MC68000 V/68	VAX-11/780 UNIX V
ltoa V1 (actual)	11100.	18400.	928.	288.
ltoa V2 (actual)	4920.	8020.	942.	291.
improvement over V1	56%	56%	-1%	-1%

Using char instead of single bit

The previous example showed how we can improve efficiency by using a smaller data type in the calculations. Let us next look at a case where moving to a larger data representation can speed the execution of a program.

Since C does not contain a Boolean type, programmers are often faced with the question of how best to represent an arrays of variables which take only Boolean values.

Let us start with the most compact form, storing each Boolean value in a single bit. Since we want to handle Boolean arrays of arbitrary size, we cannot use the bit-fields which are available in structures. We can, however, declare an array of char and then pack eight Boolean entries into each character in the array. (Some machines have more than eight bits in a char, but portability is simplified by using just eight.) The following shows a set of macros to set, clear and test an arbitrary Boolean value in the array. The arguments to the macros are the name of the array (barr) which is being used to hold the Boolean values, and the index (index) which ranges from 0 to the number of Boolean entries.

These macros assume that the index into the Boolean array is always positive. Using this fact we replace a division by 8 with a right shift of 3, and we replace a remainder operation (to identify the bit within the char) by a bitwise AND.

```
#define SETTRUE(barr, index)  (barr[(index)>>3] |= (1 << ((index) & 0x7)))
#define SETFALSE(barr, index) (barr[(index)>>3] &= ~(1 << ((index) & 0x7)))
#define TEST(barr, index)     ((barr[(index)>>3] & (1 << ((index) & 0x7)) != 0)
```

The above macros give a very compact way of storing an array of Boolean values; however, there is considerable computational overhead (ANDs, ORs and shifts) involved in setting, clearing, and testing each element of the Boolean array. We can avoid much of the overhead involved in accessing and testing the Boolean values by storing a single Boolean value in each element of a char array. (In the Plum Hall system of defined-types, these are tbool — "tiny Boolean" — elements.) This increases the size required to store the array of Booleans eight-fold, but it eliminates the shiftings, ANDing and ORing operations from each access to an element of the array of Boolean values. We are able to replace the SETTRUE, SETFALSE, and TEST macros with the following:

```
#define SETTRUE(barr, index)  (barr[index] = 1)
#define SETFALSE(barr, index) (barr[index] = 0)
#define TEST(barr, index)     (barr[index])
```

In this version, we would change the declaration

```
char boolbits[NUMBOOLS/8 + 1];
```

to

```
tbool boolbits[NUMBOOLS];
```

or

```
char boolbits[NUMBOOLS];    /* : boolean */
```

to allocate the correct sized array of Booleans.

We timed the packed and unpacked versions of the macros, with these results:

boolbits.tbl:

	8088/PC Lattice	PDP-11/23 WSL	MC68000 UNIX V	VAX-11/780 UNIX V
SETTRUE-packed	36.4	44.8	16.9	13.0
SETFALSE-packed	38.4	49.3	17.4	13.4
TEST-packed	37.7	48.4	13.7	10.7
SETTRUE-unpacked	6.87	16.5	6.28	4.12
SETFALSE-unpacked	6.87	15.3	6.28	3.30
TEST-unpacked	5.24	11.0	5.73	2.27

From these results we see that the packed Booleans were two to five times slower than the unpacked version.

4.3 Using the Register Storage Class

In most environments, the most significant simple modification of a program is the addition of the register storage class to key integer variables. As we saw in the timings of Chapter 2, the use of register storage class on the operands of an operator can have a significant impact on how long that operation takes.

In general, this improvement is seen because the compiler keeps a register variable in a high speed register. It usually saves the time required to load the variable into a register before an operation takes place, and it allows the faster "register" version of the generated machine code to be performed.

Due to a limited number of registers available for register variables on most current computers we must be selective in specifying the register storage class. The Whitesmiths 2.3 compiler for the PDP-11 allows three register variables per function; the System V/68 compiler for the 68000 allows six registers for data and four registers for pointers; the UNIX System V compiler for the VAX allows a total of six registers.

Note that some compilers simply ignore the register specification. In this case the programmer has neither gained nor lost from the addition of the register specifier. Among our example environments, the Lattice 2.15 compiler behaves in this fashion.

Note also that the keyword register may be ignored if the compiler cannot generate code for the specified data type. On many small machines, register long might be treated as auto long, if no registers can hold a long int. In recent C compilers, register char (for example) is treated as auto char if machine registers cannot faithfully model a true char variable. For these reasons, the forms that are most likely to produce the desired efficiency result are register int and register unsigned int.

Although the arbitrary use of the register storage class can, in general, do no harm (when compared with not using it at all), it is important to review the algorithm enough to determine which variables receive heavy use. These are the ones which should receive the register storage class first. Only after these have been specified should others be considered (if there are remaining registers available for register variables). The blind placement of register specifications on all integer variables may cause key variables to be locked out of registers, because lightly-used variables may be using all of the available registers.

Most compilers allocate register variables in the order in which they are declared. If more are declared than can be put into registers, the ones encountered last will receive ordinary automatic storage. To obtain the best efficiency in the widest range of environments, you should declare register variables in their order of importance.

4.4 Efficient Loops

Loops which count to zero rather than up to some value are, in general, slightly faster. The hardware in modern computers typically provides a special instruction which is a comparison of a value with zero. This special test instruction is smaller and/or faster than the generalized comparison instruction. Thus, we would expect

```
/* loop 1 .. 10 - version 1 */
short i;

for (i = 1; i <= 10; ++i)
    ;
```

to be slightly slower than

```
/* loop 10 times, while > 0 - version 2 */
short i;

for (i = 10; i > 0; --i)
    ;
```

In the Lattice 2.15 (8088) environment, there was no difference. In the other environments, there was a small difference, as expected. If we put the loop variable into register storage, there is a more substantial improvement in all environments except Lattice 2.15 (where registers are optimized without concern for register declarations):

```
/* loop 10 times, while > 0 - version 3 */
register int i;

for (i = 10; i > 0; --i)
    ;
```

The final transformation involves two changes: First, the decrement is done on the test expression itself. Second, since this decrements the loop variable one extra time, the initialization must be increased by one. Putting the decrement on the test expression can improve the speed by eliminating a separate "test" instruction in the generated code. Since the details of the resulting loop are somewhat messy, we have made a macro for the loop:

```
#define LOOPDN(a, b)   for (a = (b)+1; --a > 0; )
```

(The test is "greater than" rather than "greater than or equal to" because if a is unsigned, the test a >= 0 is always true; there is no "one-too-far" value to stop the loop.) The fourth version of the loop looks like this:

```
/* loop 10 times, with LOOPDN - version 4 */
register int i;

LOOPDN(i, 10)
    ;
```

Here are the execution results:

	8088/PC Lattice	PDP-11/23 WSL	MC68000 V/68	VAX-11/780 UNIX V
1: loop 1..10	209.	194.	75.5	33.1
2: loop 10 > 0	209.	175.	69.9	32.5
3: register > 0	209.	89.4	44.5	18.7
4: LOOPDN	206.	68.4	39.9	11.3
improvement, 4 vs 1	1%	65%	47%	66%

One final advantage of using a macro such as LOOPDN for specifying time-critical iterations is that if some environment provides a form which is even faster, the macro itself can be revised, rather than searching for all instances in the code. For this reason, the LOOPDN macro is part of the Plum Hall local.h header.

4.5 Macros vs Functions

Macros play an important role in the writing of efficient programs because they allow us to create in-line code for small, commonly-used operations. Replacing function calls with macro invocations typically has two effects. First, the resulting code is larger because the function call is now replaced by the entire operation. Second, the code is faster because there is no overhead for the function call (including pushing arguments on the stack), function entry, and function exit.

There are some cases where macros save both time and space. This is true in small functions where the code to push the arguments and do the function call is larger than the code to do the actual work of the function. In many other cases, the macro version will produce just a few bytes more code while being several times faster. Many of the "standard" C library routines, such as isdigit or isupper are often implemented as macros for this reason.

The bitcnt function is a good example. When we last saw it in Chapter 3, the code inside the function had been reduced to the single expression bitsum[x & BYTEMASK]. The appropriate macro version could look like this:

```
bitcnt.h(#6):
    /* bitcnt.h - header for bitcnt macro */
    #define BYTEMASK 0xFF
    #define bitcnt(c) (bitsum[(c) & BYTEMASK])
    extern char bitsum[];
```

Here are the experimental results:

	8088/PC Lattice	PDP-11/23 WSL	MC68000 V/68	VAX-11/780 UNIX V
bitcnt V1 (actual)	411.	455.	189.	86.9
bitcnt V5 (actual)	58.3	50.1	26.7	20.6
bitcnt V6 (actual)	11.8	12.2	9.13	3.10
improvement V6 vs V1	97%	97%	95%	96%
V1-V5 bytes per call	8	10	14	11
V6 bytes per macro	13	10	28	16

Notice that, while we obtain the efficiency advantages of placing the code in-line, we have maintained the readability and modularity which was the impetus for making a separate function in the first place.

There are some restrictions that must be followed for reliable use of macros. (The following points are summarized from Plum [1985].)

An *unsafe macro* is one whose definition does not evaluate each macro argument exactly once. We suggest giving unsafe macros names in upper-case letters, and making sure that invocations of unsafe macros contain no side-effects on the arguments.

An *expression macro* is one which expands to produce a valid C expression, and can thus be used in place of a function call. The important syntactic restriction upon expression macros is that they cannot have local variables. This may mean that auxiliary arguments may be needed for temporary results, as in the SWAP macro:

```
#define SWAP(a, b, t) ((t) = (a), (a) = (b), (b) = (t))
```

The SWAP macro illustrates the "generic" possibilities of macros: a "generic" macro can accept arguments of any compatible data types, since the compiler actually sees the expanded code. Thus, SWAP can be used to swap chars, ints, doubles, etc.

A *statement macro* can have local variables, since it produces a compound statement:

```
#define SWAP_SHORT(a, b) {short _t; _t = (a); (a) = (b); (b) = _t;}
```

The macro is no longer generic, however, and in one particular context, braces are required around the invocation:

```
if (a[i] < a[j])
    {
    SWAP_SHORT(a[i], a[j]);
    }
else
    /* ... */
```

The braces are needed because the macro itself produces a compound statement and the customary semicolon becomes a second (null) statement. Since a statement macro does not generate a single-expression result, it can only be used in a void-function context.

If a function must be referenced from assembler language or another language (e.g., Pascal), then the function can not be replaced by a macro. Functions have an address which can be referenced, while macros become in-line code which has no independent identity. This, if the algorithm requires that a pointer to the function be used (e.g., to be placed in a table or passed as an argument) then the function can not be replaced by a macro.

It is possible that a function call will be more time efficient than a macro. If the function arguments can go into registers and the function performs a substantial computation the function can save time over in-line code just by making effective use of the machine registers. Macros, in general, are not going to have an environment where they can make use of registers, although if the arguments to the macro are register variables, the generated code will be faster.

We have noted many limitations on macros. This has not been to discourage their use but rather to help ensure effective, correct use of the macros. The fact remains that macros remain an important and effective tool for improving the time efficiency of a program.

4.6 Subscripts and Pointers

C allows (in fact defines) a very close relationship between subscripted array references and pointer references. The interchangeability of these two ways of referencing data leads to another time efficiency improvement opportunity.

If repeated use is made of a particular element (or group of elements) in an array, then it is frequently faster to set a pointer to the element being referenced and then use the pointer in later calculations.

This can eliminate the recalculation of the subscript expression in every reference. To keep the comparisons simple, we will use register storage for all pointers and subscripts. The first example is a two-subscript loop over a 10 by 10 array of ints:

```
int a[10][10];
register int i, j;

for (i = 0; i < 10; ++i)
    for (j = 0; j < 10; --j)
        a[i][j] = 0;
```

Second, we will change to a single-subscript loop over a 100-element array:

```
int a[100];
register int i;

for (i = 0; i < 100; ++i)
    a[i] = 0;
```

Third, we use a pointer:

```
int a[100];
register int *p;

for (p = a; p < a + 100; ++p)
    *p = 0;
```

Fourth, we combine the increment with the indirection:

```
int a[100];
register int *p;

for (p = a; p < a + 100; )
    *p++ = 0;
```

Notice that the timings for the third and fourth versions would be exactly the same if the original two-dimensional array were being indexed:

```
int a[10][10];
register int *p;

for (p = (int *)a; p < (int *)(a + 10); )
    *p++ = 0;
```

Here are the experimental results:

	8088/PC Lattice	PDP-11/23 WSL	MC68000 V/68	VAX 11/780 UNIX V
1: 2-dim subscript	7970.	5870.	1860.	1320.
2: 1-dim subscript	3320.	2240.	1130.	350.
3: pointer *p = 0	3320.	2020.	817.	310.
4: pointer *p++ = 0	3320.	1660.	726.	272.
improvement, 4 vs 1	58%	71%	61%	79%
improvement, 4 vs 2	0%	26%	36%	22%

In these figures we see a dramatic improvement from replacing a two-subscript loop with either a single subscript or a pointer, and a small improvement from replacing a single subscript with a pointer. From these results, and other similar findings, we suggest two general rules: First, multiple subscripts are usually worth re-structuring wherever efficiency is an issue. Second, replacing a single register subscript with a pointer is warranted only under the most severe time constraints, since the subscript version is often more readable.

4.7 Profiling an Executable Program

After an algorithm has been implemented into an executable program, one further technique can be useful in identifying opportunities for optimization: the technique of dynamic *profiling*. UNIX systems have provided profilers since the early 1970's, and more recently, profilers have been written for numerous other environments.

The technique is much the same in any environment: The program is compiled with a special compilation flag, which causes the generation of code which counts the number of times each function is entered, along with other code which periodically samples the machine program counter to determine which function is currently executing. After execution of the program, a profile reporting command can be executed to produce a tabulation of results.

For an example of a program to profile, here is an implementation of the "quicksort" algorithm. This version is adapted from Bentley [1984a]; the specific implementation with "generic pointers" is as shown in Plum [1985].

```
qsortpro.c:
    /* qsort - sort array a (dimension n) using quicksort
     * based on Bentley, CACM April 84
     * Comments use notation A[i], a (fictitious) array of things
     * that are of size elt_size.
     */
    #include "local.h"
    /* swapfn - swap  elt_size bytes  a <--> b (internal routine)
     */
    void swapfn(a, b, elt_size)
        register char *a;   /* pointer to one element of A */
        register char *b;   /* pointer to another element of A */
        size_t elt_size;    /* size of each element */
        {
        register size_t i;
        char tmp;

        LOOPDN(i, elt_size)
            {
            SWAP(*a, *b, tmp);
            ++a, ++b;
            }
        }

    /* iqsort - internal quicksort routine */
    void iqsort(p_lo, p_hi, elt_size, cmpfn)
        char *p_lo;         /* ptr to low element of (sub)array */
        char *p_hi;         /* ptr to high element of (sub)array */
        size_t elt_size;    /* size of each element */
        int (*cmpfn)();     /* comparison function ptr */
        {
        char *p_mid;                /* pointer to middle element */
        register char *p_i;         /* pointer to A[i] */
        register char *p_lastlo;    /* pointer to A[lastlo] */

        if (p_hi <= p_lo)           /* is partition trivial? */
            return;
        p_mid = p_lo + ((((p_hi - p_lo) / elt_size) / 2) * elt_size);
        swapfn(p_lo, p_mid, elt_size);  /* pick the middle element as pivot */
        p_lastlo = p_lo;
        for (p_i = p_lo + elt_size;  p_i <= p_hi; p_i += elt_size)
            {
            if ((*cmpfn)(p_lo, p_i) > 0)
                {
                p_lastlo += elt_size;
                swapfn(p_lastlo, p_i, elt_size);
                }
            }
        swapfn(p_lo, p_lastlo, elt_size);
        iqsort(p_lo, p_lastlo - elt_size, elt_size, cmpfn);
        iqsort(p_lastlo + elt_size, p_hi, elt_size, cmpfn);
        }
```

```
/* qsort - the callable entry point */
void qsort(a, n, size, pf)
    data_ptr a;      /* address of array A to be sorted */
    size_t n;        /* number of elements in A */
    size_t size;     /* size of each element */
    int (*pf)();     /* comparison function ptr */
    {
    iqsort((data_ptr)a, (char *)a + (n-1) * size, size, pf);
    }

/* qsortm - test the qsort function */
static int a[100] =
    {
     0,  1,  2,  3,  4,  5,  6,  7,  8,  9,
    10, 11, 12, 13, 14, 15, 16, 17, 18, 19,
    20, 21, 22, 23, 24, 25, 26, 27, 28, 29,
    30, 31, 32, 33, 34, 35, 36, 37, 38, 39,
    40, 41, 42, 43, 44, 45, 46, 47, 48, 49,
    50, 51, 52, 53, 54, 55, 56, 57, 58, 59,
    60, 61, 62, 63, 64, 65, 66, 67, 68, 69,
    70, 71, 72, 73, 74, 75, 76, 77, 78, 79,
    80, 81, 82, 83, 84, 85, 86, 87, 88, 89,
    90, 91, 92, 93, 94, 95, 96, 97, 98, 99,
    };

/* intcmp - compare two ints */
int intcmp(pi, pj)
    register int *pi, *pj;
    {
    if (*pi < *pj)
        return (-1);
    else if (*pi == *pj)
        return (0);
    else
        return (1);
    }

/* qsortm (main) - run the test */
main(ac, av)
    int ac;
    char *av[];
    {
    int i;

    for (i = 1; i <= 1000; ++i)
        qsort((data_ptr)a, 100, sizeof(int), intcmp);
    }
```

When the program is compiled for profiling and then executed, the prof utility produces the following output (on the VAX 11/780, in this case):

```
qsortpro.out:
```

%Time	Seconds	Cumsecs	#Calls	msec/call	Name
33.3	16.37	16.37	127000	0.1289	_iqsort
30.8	15.17	31.53	345000	0.0440	_swapfn
20.2	9.95	41.48	480000	0.0207	_intcmp
7.2	3.53	45.02	126002	0.0280	udiv
5.6	2.73	47.75	1	2733.	_main
2.8	1.37	49.12			mcount
0.1	0.05	49.17	1000	0.050	_qsort
0.0	0.00	49.17	2	0.	_profil
0.0	0.00	49.17	1	0.	_getenv
0.0	0.00	49.17	1	0.	_strcpy
0.0	0.00	49.17	2	0.	_monitor
0.0	0.00	49.17	1	0.	_creat
0.0	0.00	49.17	1	0.	_write

The columns (from left to right) give the percentage of time spent in each function, the number of seconds spent in each function, the cumulative total of seconds, the number of calls to each function, the number of milliseconds per function call, and the name of each function. One typical observation from such information is to notice that the program spends about a third of its time in the swapfn function. Each call to swapfn takes about 44 microseconds. (Look in the msec/call column.) Recalling from Chapter 2 that a function call with three arguments takes about 22.4 microseconds on the VAX, we could eliminate about half the swapping time by changing the function calls to in-line code, for a net improvement of about 15% in total execution time.

There are some cautions to observe in interpreting profile results. There is usually some round-off in the determination of execution addresses, so small functions may not be accurately represented in the time samples. The times reported for the seldom-executed functions are subject to the errors associated with small samples. (This is usually little problem, because we are interested in the functions that take the most time.) If one function is called from several other functions, there is no way to determine what proportion of its time to attribute to each of the calling functions. In other words, the profiler always gives information about the lowest function in the current calling hierarchy.

We will not pursue any optimizations of this quicksort implementation. This version has greater problems with stack-space usage than it does with execution time, so we will revisit the program in Chapter 7.

4.8 Unfounded Efficiency Myths

It is worth mentioning a few "techniques" which people have sometimes mistakenly believed to improve efficiency.

Programmers familiar with interpreted languages such as Basic or APL sometimes have the belief that filling a source line with multiple statements produces a faster C program. This will, however, have no effect on execution time in any C environment that we know of. It is also considered poor programming style.

Another myth is that the conditional operator is somehow faster than the if construct, as if

```
minab = a < b ? a : b;
```

were faster than

```
if (a < b)
    minab = a;
else
    minab = b;
```

The conditional expression does have its uses; it allows expression macros to embody a choice, for example. It is not necessarily faster or slower than the equivalent if construct.

There is a common misconception that a compiler will generate better code for a test such as

```
if (i)
```

than for the test

```
if (i != 0)
```

This is simply false. The compiler has to generate code for the *implicit* test against 0 in the first case and it will generate code for the exact same test when it is explicitly written out in the second case.

Another common belief is that multiple assignments in one statement are faster. To the contrary, we found in our timing studies that

```
i = j = 255;
```

is sometimes slower than

```
i = 255;
j = 255;
```

We would recommend that the selection be based on considerations of readability rather than efficiency. If the assignments to i and j are intrinsically equal (such that a modification would necessarily affect both the same), then the first form seems preferable.

Doubtless there are other unfounded myths about efficiency. Our hope in describing empirical measurement techniques is that your decisions can be based upon real observation rather than myth.

4.9 Last Resort Techniques

This concludes our list of C-specific efficiency techniques. There are two other last-resort techniques: implement critical operations in assembler language, and get a faster processor.

Regarding assembler language, the details of interfacing C with assembler are different in each environment, and there is not enough that we can say in general about the techniques. In extremely time-critical situations, these details may need to be mastered. Even in these situations, however, it is often best to start with a C function which does the job, and use its assembler listing as a starting point. If possible, preserve the same interface, so that porting the program to another processor can start with the C version of the function. (The C version may in fact be fast enough on the new processor.)

It is, of course, a testimonial to the portability of C that projects have been able to re-target an application onto a faster processor. The remedy is severe, but when no further efficiencies can be wrung out of the code, it remains the remedy of last resort.

CHAPTER 5: MEASURING SPACE

We will now turn our attention to the issue of measuring the space requirements for C programs.

5.1 When Is Space Important

There are many environments where the amount of memory necessary to run a program is of concern and interest. The most obvious are environments where there are limitations on the available address space (i.e., the largest amount of memory which can be accessed by the processor). This is frequently a concern when working with 8-bit processors (e.g., Zilog Z80, Intel 8080, Motorola MC6809) where the total address space is limited to only 64K.

Even when the processor's address space is adequate, there may be a limit on the physical memory which is available in the system. Many real-time controllers are designed with very small memories to keep the total hardware cost low. It is frequently very expensive (relative to the total cost of the system) to add additional memory. This is becoming even more common with the growing availability and popularity of MCUs (Micro Computer Units) which contain the processor and some limited amount of memory (e.g., 8K) all on a single chip (e.g., Motorola MC68HC11). If the application can execute successfully in the on-chip memory then the cost of extra circuitry and additional memory chips is avoided.

Physical memory is also an issue when developing applications for personal computers and microprocessor-based work stations. It is usually desirable to develop products which have a broad audience, therefore you want minimum space requirements so that, although customers could buy extra memory to run the package, they won't have to. This is particularly true for systems software where the user must do useful work on top of the package (e.g., a "windowing" package), but it is generally true for almost all applications.

Even when the address space and memory are available, there may be limitations on how much of the memory can be accessed. Many popular C compilers for the IBM-PC and PC compatibles only support programs which run in a "small" model (i.e., 64K program space, 64K data space). Many of those that support larger models (up to 1M program and 1M data), such as Lattice C, generate code which is less efficient.

In rare cases, size is even a concern on large systems. On systems with virtual memory and huge program address spaces, there is still a cost penalty associated with large programs, including the time to page portions of the program in and out. This becomes a major concern if the program frequently jumps from one section to another, in which case frequent page swapping may cause a degradation in performance.

On newer hardware, the size of a loop may have a direct bearing on how fast it executes. Many of the newer processors (e.g., Motorola MC68020) keep an on-chip instruction cache and can execute a tight loop very quickly, because they only fetch the instructions from memory one time and then use them out of the cache for the rest of the loop. (The 68020 cache is 256 bytes long.) This technique only works for loops which completely fit within the cache. If the loop sequence is too long, then normal (slower) processing is done.

In any environment, understanding the space utilization is useful when determining where and when to make time/space tradeoffs. For example, if a program is well within the space limitations, it may be worth replacing a function with a table of precomputed values.

Before we discuss the details of how to measure the size of our programs, it is useful to understand the C language view of the memory where the program will execute.

5.2 Memory and a C Program

The C language views a program's memory as being divided up into three pieces, *text* (also called *program* in some documentation), *data*, and *dynamic*. In simple terms, the *text* area is for program code (instructions). The *data* area is for static variables and data. The *dynamic* area is for the automatic variables, the "heap" (for dynamic allocation), and for function-call bookkeeping. The following figure shows a conceptual model of the memory layout for a program.

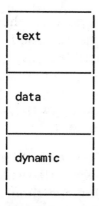

Besides the instructions which make up the program, other items may be placed into the text area. Constant items such as strings, jump tables for switch statements, and floating point constants are occasionally also allocated in the text area. The text section is not modifiable, so it could be placed in ROM if this was useful or necessary.

Data objects which have a lifetime that persists for the entire program are placed in the *data* area. In many implementations, strings, floating point constants, and switch tables are also placed in this area. Some implementations have an option on the compiler giving the user control over the placement of some of these items in either the text or data areas (e.g., Whitesmiths C).

The data area is sometimes divided into two sections, an area for explicitly initialized data and an area for "uninitialized" global and static data. This division has its historic roots in the fact that UNIX object modules make a distinction between these two types of data; the initialized area is known as the *data segment* and the uninitialized area is known as the *bss segment*. The initialization (to the default zero) of the bss segment is stored in a very compact form in the object module, while the initializers for the (initialized) data segment contain each individual initializer.

The dynamic area includes automatic variables, function housekeeping information, and storage which is used when objects are created using the memory allocation routines (e.g., malloc and calloc).

The dynamic area is often divided into two sections. The first is the *stack*. The stack is the area where automatic variables are dynamically allocated for each function when the function is invoked.

The stack is also the area where, in almost all systems, the actual arguments are pushed for function calls. A few systems (such as the VAX) also include a count of the number of arguments on this call. When the function call is made the return address is pushed onto the stack. Function housekeeping information is also pushed onto the stack when the called function is entered. As a minimum the calling procedure's pointer to its local data (its *frame pointer*) is saved, so that it can be restored when control is returned.

The stack is also where compiler-generated temporaries (used during complex computations and some optimizations) are kept.

The second part of the dynamic data area is the *heap*, where user-controlled dynamic space allocations take place. When structures like linked lists or binary trees are built by a program, the space for these structures comes from the heap area. The allocation and freeing of space in the heap is not tied to function entry and exit. It is under the programmer's control.

In some environments (e.g., the one used by the standard C in UNIX System V), the stack and heap share a single memory area, with the stack growing from one end and the heap growing from the other. In this type of environment the program can run as long as the sum of the stack and the heap does not exceed the available memory.

Other environments (e.g., Lattice C on MS-DOS), allocate separate and distinct areas for the stack and heap. This means that it is possible to run out of stack space while there is still remaining space in the heap (and vice versa). The decision to structure the run-time environment in this way was made to accommodate some other desirable facilities. However, it does put more responsibility on the developer to understand how the dynamic data space is being used.

5.3 Measuring Program Space Requirements

Now that we have a little background on how a program's memory is laid out let us look at some ways of measuring the amount of space actually used by a program.

Let us start by looking at the size of the text and static data areas. The dynamic data area is much more difficult to estimate, so we will leave that for a later discussion.

All of the systems that we are aware of supply some way of determining how big the text and static data areas are. On UNIX systems the size command is used for this purpose. It produces section size information for an object file, producing four numbers. These are the size of the text area, the static initialized data (referred to as data), the static uninitialized data (referred to as bss), and the total of these three sections.

In the examples of this section, we will use the qsortpro.c program from Chapter 4 as our example program (compiled *without* profiling). On the VAX UNIX system, we obtained size information by executing this command::

```
$ cc -o qsortpro.x qsortpro.c
$ size qsortpro.x
508 + 404 + 0 = 912
```

This tells us that the text area takes 508 bytes (decimal), the (initialized) data area takes 404 bytes, and the uninitialized data area ("bss") takes zero bytes, for a total of 912 bytes. (The measurement includes library functions and everything else in the executable file.)

On systems which do not supply the size command or its equivalent, there are several possibilities. Some compilers, such as Lattice 2.15, the compile step reveals the text and data size of the resulting object module:

```
Module size P=01B0 D=00CA
```

which (after converting the hex numbers) tells us that QSORTPRO.OBJ takes 432 bytes of text space and 202 bytes of data space. (These sizes are for the object file only, without library.)

If we want to find out about the space used by each function in the executable program, we can make use of a "link map." This listing, which may be produced by the linker or another utility, can be used to find the locations (usually relative to a starting point of 0) where each of the global symbols (functions and variables) can be found. Each of the symbols is normally labeled as residing in one of the sections (e.g., text, initialized static data, uninitialized static data).

On UNIX systems, the link map is generated by the nm command. Using the same program as in the previous example, the output from nm looks something like this (abbreviated) version:

```
Symbols from qsortpro.x:

Name                  Value   Class  Section

start            |        0|extern|.text
mcount           |       58|extern|.text
_swapfn          |       60|extern|.text
_iqsort          |      112|extern|.text
_qsort           |      312|extern|.text
_intcmp          |      352|extern|.text
_main            |      388|extern|.text
udiv             |      452|extern|.text
_exit            |      492|extern|.text
__cleanup        |      504|extern|.text
_environ         |      512|extern|.data
_a               |      516|static|.data
_etext           |      508|extern|
_edata           |      916|extern|
_end             |      916|extern|
```

Note first of all that all the external names produced by C have been prefixed with an underscore. We will follow this naming convention while we discuss the nm output.

The functions from our qsortpro.c source file are reported to have these addresses in the text area: _swapfn is at 60, _iqsort at 112, _qsort at 312, _intcmp at 352, and _main at 388. Just after _main comes udiv at 452, so our functions take 452 - 60, or 392 bytes of the text area. The symbol _etext stands for "end of text," so the entire text area is reported to contain 508 bytes (just as the size command reported). Subtracting 392 from 508 tells us that the other library code takes 116 bytes. (Had we called any I/O, the library would have been much larger.)

On MS-DOS, the /MAP option on the link command will produce a link map. Here is the link map for QSORTPRO.EXE:

```
Start   Stop    Length  Name            Class
00000H  00001H  0002H   BASE            PROG
00002H  01F61H  1F60H   PROG            PROG
01F62H  01F63H  0002H   TAIL            PROG
01F70H  0287DH  090EH   DATA            DATA
02880H  028FFH  0080H   STACK           DATA

Address             Publics by Name

0000:0C3D           ALLMEM
01F7:01AC           ARGC
01F7:01AE           ARGV
        ... etc ...

Address             Publics by Value

0000:0207           XCABT
0000:0220           XCOVF
0000:023C           XCEXIT
0000:0255           SWAPFN
0000:0297           IQSORT
0000:0357           QSORT
0000:0388           INTCMP
0000:03C8           MAIN
0000:0405           LSBRK
        ... etc ...
```

The code for our source file can be located in the second listing ("publics by value"); it extends from 255 (hex) to 405 (hex), for a total of 1B0 (hex), or 432 (decimal), just as the Lattice compiler reported earlier. At the top of the link map is an overall space report, which says that the PROG (i.e., text) area takes 1F60 (hex) or 8032 (decimal) bytes. The executable file itself is quite large, because most of the I/O library is included by default. (This environment, like many others of its type, provides a special means to dispense with the I/O library when it is not wanted.)

To summarize, we have seen that each environment provides some means to determine the size (text and data bytes) of each object file, and of each function in the final executable program. We now turn to the more difficult subject of dynamic memory requirements.

5.4 Measuring Dynamic Memory Requirements

There is no way of statically determining exactly how much dynamic data space will be used by an arbitrary C program. C language features, such as recursion and conditional dynamic allocation, make a complete analysis of many programs, independent of the input data, impossible. Despite this limitation in the general case, there is quite a bit that can be done when certain restrictions hold and good test data is available.

As we noted in the introduction to this chapter, the size issue is primarily of concern in environments where the available space may be limited due to address space limitations or physical memory limitations. For this reason we will concentrate on approaches to determining the size of the dynamic data space which will work in these environments, with the compilers that are available.

The Execute-and-See Approach

The authors are unaware of any systems which will directly supply a way of monitoring the amount of stack and heap used; however, we frequently can find out a lot by indirect means. We will begin by looking at stack usage only.

If three conditions hold, then there exists a simple way of measuring how much stack space is necessary for a program to successfully execute.

These conditions are:

1.   We have one or more good test cases which thoroughly exercise the program and test the limits of its requirements for memory.

2.   The compiler being used supports run-time stack checking. (The compiler does this by adding code which is executed during function entry to check the current state of the stack.)

3.   There is a means to specify how large the stack area for a program will be.

The first requirement is placed upon the developer. It is important to consider situations which push the program to its largest memory requirement, not only as a way of testing the size requirements but also as a way of testing the program's handling of this extreme case. It is a useful test case even if size-testing is not being done.

The last two are conditions which are placed upon the compiler and operating system. These are being met by an increasing number of compilers on small systems. The authors are aware of several compilers which supply these capabilities including Lattice C for the IBM PC and Whitesmiths C for all of its supported environments.

If these conditions are met, the simplest way to measure the amount of stack space used by a program is to repeatedly execute the program, using the test cases as input. Each time the amount of space allocated for the stack should be reduced. Eventually, the stack-checking will detect an error because of insufficient space. The required stack space will then fall somewhere between the amount used in the last successful execution and the unsuccessful execution.

The determination of the actual amount of memory used for heap allocations is more difficult because the program typically does not have fine control over how much space will be made available (in contrast to the ability to specify a specific stack size). This is because the space for the heap is usually requested from the operating system as it is required.

One approach is to attempt to track the dynamic allocation of memory by never calling the allocation or freeing routines directly. Instead, a routine which keeps a running total and high water mark of the amount of space which is being requested and freed by the program is always used. This routine then always make the appropriate library allocation or free call. While this approach seems attractive at first, there are several problems with it.

The first is that library routines, which are beyond the control of the programmer, may allocate and free space on the heap. Library requirements for control blocks and buffers will not be tracked by this approach. Second, the total size required may not be a simple adding of the allocations with appropriate subtractions for frees. The actual space allocations may be made in some minimum block size. Each allocation of memory may also have some overhead memory associated with it which is used to link the blocks for garbage collection when the blocks are freed. Furthermore, holes may develop in the allocated memory. There may be several small holes which, when totalled, may be sufficient to meet an allocation request but which are unusable because of the requirement to allocate a single request as a contiguous block.

These problems make this approach a very rough estimate of the actual memory requirements, at best.

A better approach can be used if several conditions are met. If you are able to determine the stack usage requirements using the technique discussed previously and you are also able to determine the total amount of memory which is available to the program, then it is possible to determine how much heap space is required by the program.

The first step is to determine how much space is required for the text and static data areas of the program. This is done by using the size (or equivalent) command or the link map, as was discussed earlier. After this is determined, the stack requirements are evaluated using the technique in the previous section. We now know how much space is used by everything except the heap.

Since there are no options (that we are aware of) for specifying a limit on the amount of heap space which is to be allocated, the best way of controlling the heap size is to reduce the total available memory in a controlled way. This can be done by allocating an array of the desired size to "tie up" a block of memory.

The approach to testing the size of the heap is to repeatedly execute the program, using the test cases as input. Each time the size of the allocated array should be increased. Eventually, some allocation request will cause an error because of insufficient space.

Some Other Approaches

If the above techniques do not work because stack checking or control of the stack size is not available, then other, more limited techniques can be used.

If you are working in a dedicated emulator environment (i.e. you have control over all of memory and the processor at the beginning of a program's execution) then a fairly simple technique can be used.

First, you must determine what area of memory will be used for the stack and heap. In environments where emulators are used this is frequently done via special global variables (see your compiler documentation) or via directives to the linker which is generating the load module.

Once you know the area of memory which will be used, fill this area with a pattern of bytes which is unlikely to occur naturally in the data of the program. You then run the program. After the execution is complete, you need to examine the memory block to determine the range of locations where the pattern has been overwritten for the stack and the range for the heap. The sum of these two areas is the total dynamic data space required.

If these empirical approaches (like stack-checking) are not available, the developer must find some way of estimating. That is the topic of the next chapter.

CHAPTER 6: ESTIMATION OF SPACE REQUIREMENTS

All of the techniques presented in the previous chapter assumed that there was sufficient memory to run the program on the test system and that the size determination was primarily intended to determine if the program could be run on a similar system with less available memory. This is not always the case.

It is often most useful to do size estimations before a program is developed. In fact, size estimation pays its greatest dividends when applied early to a large software effort. Large efforts are notorious for resulting in programs that far exceed the specifications for size. If it is possible to determine the memory requirements for a software system early in a development, then informed decisions can be made if the system is going to be too large (e.g., functionality changes, algorithm and data structure changes). The end of a project, when space overruns are usually discovered, is frequently too late. It is very costly to have to discard or rewrite large pieces of code because they will not run in the desired target system.

Even if there is flexibility in the total amount of memory which can be made available to a program, it is frequently necessary in engineering environments to decide early in the design cycle how much memory to include in a hardware design. This early decision is made just when the least amount is known about the size of the program. Experience and estimation techniques are the best tools for answering these space estimation questions.

Let's look at each part of the the C program memory.

6.1 Text Estimation

In Chapter 3 we introduced a collection of routines which were used to measure the time for each of the basic operators and statements in C. These routines were also used to produce size tables for each of the operators and statements. The following pages will show the results of these measurements.

In these tables, you will notice that each operator of C takes a few bytes of machine code. A few operators take no code at all. For example, the conversion of an int to a char usually takes no extra instructions. Some of the operators take only one or two bytes. An "average" is probably meaningless without specifying the nature of the program, but to an order of magnitude the "average" is something like ten bytes. The most expensive operators involve floating-point operations on machines without FPP support. Here, sizes of forty or fifty bytes are found in some cases.

To generalize this last observation, any operation that is not directly supported by the machine hardware takes significantly more space. This includes floating-point without FPP support, long arithmetic on machines without 32-bit registers, and the tests and conditionals.

The tests and conditionals generate more code because we are measuring the calculation of an actual 0 or 1 result. As mentioned in Section 2.6, the computation of

```
i = j < k;
```

involves very much the same code as the control structure

```
if (j < k)
    i = 1;
else
    i = 0;
```

Indeed, the generated assembler code often looks very much like this. As we mentioned in Section 2.6, we need not count any extra code for the if itself when estimating space, because the space is already accounted for in the test expression itself.

These tables are not presented with any idea that you would want to memorize any of their details. Read them for the general patterns that they reveal, to give yourself an intuitive feel for the type of code that representative C compilers produce.

Code space table for Lattice 2.15 on 8088:

```
space.88:
    8088/PC  Lattice 2.15 MS-DOS
    Small model
```

Operation	short (1)	char (2)	long (3)	double (4)	float (5)
s.m	0	0	0	0	0
p->m	3	5	3	29	23
a[k]	8	10	8	-	-
(double)k	8	10	11	0	11
(long)k	7	9	0	12	6
(int)k	0	2	0	12	6
(char)k	2	2	2	14	8
&k	0	0	0	0	0
~k	2	4	7	-	-
++k	4	8	15	33	30
k++	3	14	11	-	-
!k	10	10	12	29	27
-k	2	4	10	17	14
j * k	3	17	12	21	39
j / k	4	18	12	21	39
j % k	4	18	12	-	-
j + k	3	9	9	21	39
j - k	3	9	9	21	39
j << k	5	11	16	-	-
j >> k	5	11	16	-	-
j <= k	12	18	21	33	51
j != k	12	18	20	33	51
j && k	16	16	20	46	38
j || k	16	16	20	46	38
j & k	3	9	9	-	-
j | k	3	9	9	-	-
j ^ k	3	9	9	-	-
i ? j : k	11	13	19	31	29
j = k	6	6	12	12	12

(1) short, int, unsigned int (2) char (3) long (4) double (5) float

Code space table for Whitesmiths 2.3 on PDP-11/23:

```
space.23:
   Code space for operators
   PDP 11/23 Whitesmiths 2.3 Idris
```

Operation	register (1)	short (2)	long (3)	(FPP) double (4)	(no FPP) double (5)
s.m	-	2	2	-	-
p->m	4	6	6	-	-
a[k]	8	10	10	-	-
(double)k	12	14	16	0	0
(long)k	4	6	2	12	12
(int)k	0	2	4	6	14
(char)k	0	2	4	6	14
&k	-	6	6	6	6
~k	4	6	12	-	-
++k	2	6	12	12	14
k++	4	8	18	-	-
!k	12	14	22	14	2
-k	4	6	14	2	32
j * k	4	8	22	4	38
j / k	6	10	22	4	38
j % k	6	10	22	-	-
j + k	4	8	18	4	38
j - k	4	8	18	4	38
j << k	4	8	12	-	-
j >> k	8	12	20	-	-
j <= k	12	16	34	18	14
j != k	12	16	34	18	14
j && k	16	20	36	22	8
j || k	16	20	36	22	8
j & k	8	12	24	-	-
j | k	4	8	16	-	-
j ^ k	4	10	20	-	-
i ? j : k	10	16	32	14	56
j = k	2	6	12	8	24

```
(1) register int
(2) short, unsigned short, int, unsigned int, char, unsigned char
(3) long (4) double, float (with FPP) (5) double, float (no FPP)

Note: for float (no FPP) add an average of 20 bytes per operand
      to the space shown for double ops
```

Code space table for UNIX System V/68 on 68000:

```
space.68k:
     Code space for operators
     68000 System V/68
     10MHz, 1 wait state
     No floating point processor
```

Operation	register (1)	auto (2)	static (3)	double (4)	float (5)
s.m	-	6	8	-	-
p->m	4	10	12	-	-
a[k]	10	14	18	-	-
(double)k	4	8	10	0	6
(long)k	0	6	8	14	10
(int)k	0	6	8	14	10
(char)k	6	8	10	18	14
&k	-	6	6	6	6
~k	4	8	10	-	-
++k	2	10	14	32	46
k++	4	10	14	-	-
!k	14	16	18	30	26
-k	4	8	10	10	12
j * k	10	8	12	20	40
j / k	10	20	24	20	40
j % k	10	20	24	-	-
j + k	4	14	18	20	40
j - k	4	14	18	20	40
j << k	4	12	16	-	-
j >> k	4	12	16	-	-
j <= k	14	20	24	40	60
j != k	14	20	24	40	60
j && k	20	24	28	50	42
j || k	20	24	28	50	42
j & k	4	14	18	-	-
j | k	4	14	18	-	-
j ^ k	4	14	18	-	-
i ? j : k	14	26	32	40	50
j = k	2	6	10	12	8

```
(1) register int (2) auto: long, int, short, char, and unsigned varieties
(3) static: long, int, short, char, and unsigned varieties
(4) double (5) float
```

Code space table for UNIX System V on VAX 11/780:

```
space.vax:
    Code space for operators
    VAX 11/780 UNIX System V
    With floating-point hardware
```

Operation	register (1)	long (2)	short (3)	double (4)
s.m	–	1	1	–
p->m	1	5	5	–
a[k]	2	6	6	–
(double)k	2	3	3	0
(long)k	0	1	1	4
(int)k	0	1	1	4
(char)k	3	4	4	4
&k	–	4	4	4
~k	3	4	7	–
++k	2	4	5	4
k++	2	7	7	–
!k	11	12	12	14
-k	3	4	7	3
j * k	4	6	11	5
j / k	4	6	11	5
j % k	11	15	19	–
j + k	4	6	11	5
j - k	4	6	11	5
j << k	4	6	9	–
j >> k	7	9	15	–
j <= k	12	14	14	16
j != k	12	14	14	16
j && k	15	17	17	19
j || k	15	17	17	19
j & k	7	9	14	–
j | k	4	6	11	–
j ^ k	4	6	11	–
i ? j : k	15	18	18	29
j = k	3	5	5	5

```
(1) register int (2) long, unsigned long, int, unsigned int
(3) short, unsigned short, char, unsigned char (4) double, float
```

We also measured representative code space requirements for function calls, function definitions, function returns, and "jumps" (end of loop, break, continue, and goto). With the caution that these can vary greatly in size, here are the figures:

Code space in bytes

	8088/PC Lattice	PDP-11/23 WSL	MC68000 V/68	VAX-11/780 UNIX V
Function call	3	4	4	7
Function definition	15	6	28	6
Function return	5	4	8	2
Jump	2	2	2	2

In the Lattice 2.15 8088 environment, and the System V/68 68000 environment, stack-overflow checking is generated by default in each function-definition prolog, so the space reported is therefore much greater. The Whitesmiths 2.3 compiler also supported stack-overflow checking, but as a special option. A note of caution is in order about the "jump" figures: in all these environments, the size of a jump instruction depends on several factors, primarily the distance to the target of the jump. In our small test cases, jumps were short; in larger functions they will typically be longer.

The passing of arguments and returned values takes (very) roughly the same code space as an assignment, of the appropriate storage class and type, so it does not appear in this simple table.

Having said all this, we should point out that operator-by-operator estimation of space requirements is not generally as productive as the equivalent process for time estimation. One can generally find inner loops and critical cases to help reduce the effort of time estimation, but every instruction counts the same for space. We did try some operator-by-operator space estimation, and got results accurate to about 20%. But an older rule of thumb did just as well: On previous projects, we have used "250 bytes per page of source code" as a typical attribute of our programming style and types of programs. Our utility printing program prints 56 lines to the page, so the 99-line qsortpro program would be predicted to produce 440 bytes of object text space. The actual numbers were 392 (VAX, as described in the previous chapter), 432 (8088), and 398 (PDP-11).

On some large projects, proper consideration for the thickness of paper could yield estimates in Kbytes per inch of printout. The serious side to this observation is that size estimation involves large aggregations of code. The size tables are useful for determining the effect that widespread use of register storage or different data types may have on the resulting code size, but not for operator-by-operator size counting.

6.2 Static Data Estimation

Once the major static data structures for a project have been designed it is possible to determine how much memory they will require. The simplest way to determine the size for complex structures is to actually write the C declarations for the structures and use the compiler to process them. If the target system is available then the `sizeof` operator can be used and the size of each structure can be printed out. The approach of using the compiler to determine the sizes of structures avoids possible inaccuracies which a simple adding up of the structure members might introduce. (Structures may have holes due to alignment considerations.) This inaccuracy is probably of small concern in a single structure, but when an array of structures is used, the inaccuracy is multiplied by the number of elements in the array.

The size of individual objects (e.g., `int`, `long`, `double`) are usually available in the documentation accompanying the compiler.

6.3 Dynamic Memory Estimation

Dynamic memory, as noted in the previous chapter, can be viewed as having two parts, the stack and the heap.

Stack

An estimate of the stack usage requires an understanding of the hierarchy of function calls which will be made by the program. The stack memory requirements can be determined, at least in part, by adding the local (automatic) memory requirements of all of the functions which must be active for each hierarchy in the program. The hierarchy requiring the most space determines the stack space requirement for the local variables during program.

Several additional factors must be considered in determining the stack requirements. The first is that function calls themselves take up stack space. There is stack space for the function arguments as well as several locations of housekeeping information.

In addition to this information a "fudge factor" should be included to leave room for the compiler-generated temporary locations which may needed. A small amount like 20 bytes is usually adequate, but the exact figure is implementation-dependent, and sometimes varies case-by-case. Consult your compiler manual for details.

The sum of these three pieces (local variables, function call arguments and housekeeping requirements, and compiler generated temporaries) gives a reasonable estimate of the actual stack usage. However, there are several things which must be considered.

The first issue has to do with the very limited amount of information which is available about dynamic memory usage (stack and heap) which occurs during calls to library routines (e.g., printf, sin). Whenever library routines are called, the programmer frequently has little or no insight into the stack or heap memory requirements. Unless the vendor supplies some information on these items (e.g., run-time library source listings), the program developer must resort to measuring the stack requirements using the techniques discussed in the previous chapter.

Another problem arises when dealing with recursive functions (where a function either directly or indirectly calls itself). With recursive functions, it is frequently difficult to determine how many times a function will occur in the calling hierarchy, since it may be data-dependent. This is a time when a worst-case analysis should be attempted to try to determine some upper limit on the number of times the function could be called recursively and therefore appear in a calling hierarchy. For example, the recursive implementation of quicksort (as shown in Chapter 4) is always vulnerable to some ordering of the data in which the hierarchy depth almost equals the number of array elements. (In Section 7.7 we will revise the quicksort program to use a small stack of known size.)

Another issue arises when trying to determine the actual function hierarchy which will occur during the execution of a program. A static analysis of all possible calling sequences gives a worst-case analysis of the size issue, though it may indicate a larger than actual requirement if data-dependent control flow causes some calling hierarchies never to occur.

Heap

Estimating the amount of space which will be required for the heap requires at least two pieces of information. The first is the size of each item which will be allocated and the second is the number of times it will be allocated.

The size of each of the objects can be determined by using the techniques described for static variables. It should be noted that some systems have a minimum size for each storage allocation. Therefore, the estimates for allocations for scalar items (e.g., int, long) or small structures or arrays may not be accurate. This is an issue which is very compiler-dependent. Again, consult your manual if necessary.

The number of times each allocation will be done is usually determined by the inputs to the program. An estimate of the "largest" input which will be handled should be used when determining the number of allocations which will take place.

As noted in the previous chapter, there is considerable potential for inaccurate estimates of dynamic heap space requirements. This is due to additional factors such as block housekeeping overhead and the fragmentation of available memory because of allocation and freeing patterns and garbage collection techniques. These, again, are very system-dependent issues which need to be addressed on a system by system basis.

6.4 Total Space Estimation

Once all of the pieces are determined, the total space for the program can be estimated by adding them together.

When doing early estimates for large projects, it is frequently the case that the least accurate estimates occur in the text area. To help compensate for this, it is very important that several techniques be used when space utilization is a concern.

First, each function should be given a "space budget". This gives each function a target for the amount of text and data space which it should be using. It will help each developer doing the detailed design to make informed design tradeoffs between space and size. In addition it allows an earlier tracking of space problems. If space is tracked, just as functionality is, during the development of a project, then early trouble signs can be used to initiate effective corrective action.

To avoid the problem of a programmer who is running out of space from throwing data structures and code "over the fence" into a neighbor's space, it is necessary to define exactly what a module must do.

Finally, it is important that the system architects monitor the decisions so that decisions which optimize a small piece of the program do not cause the total system to be sub-optimized. See Brooks [1975] for an entertaining account of all of these issues.

CHAPTER 7: IMPROVING SPACE EFFICIENCY

The C language provides the program developer many opportunities to improve the space efficiency of a program. We will look at some of these specific techniques and the associated C language facilities.

7.1 Using Register Variables

One of the interesting discoveries of the measurements that were done on code size had to do with the use of the register type modifier. We found that the use of register on a variable not only caused calculations which used that variable to execute more quickly, but it also caused the size of the related code (text space) to be smaller.

Operations using register variables frequently avoid the cost of loading the variable value into a register (when the variable is referenced) and storing out to memory (when the variable is assigned to).

It is also possible, on some machines, for the compiler to generate instructions for an operation which uses register operands rather than instructions which use memory locations as the operands. The register operand instructions are usually shorter and faster than the memory operand versions of the instructions.

The use of register is one of the few cases where we have both time and space savings.

7.2 Using Small Data Types

Perhaps the most obvious way to save data memory is to use data types which use less memory whenever possible.

The savings which are gained by using smaller types are most important when they are being used in arrays. For example, in each of our four representative machines an array of 1000 double elements requires 8000 bytes while a 1000-element float array takes up only 4000 bytes.

Let's look at some conditions where it is reasonable to consider using a smaller sized type than may be first considered.

When the range of a variable is limited to small non-negative numbers (i.e. < 128) then a variable of char type (which only requires one byte) can be used rather than one of the (short, "plain", or long) int types (which require at least 2 bytes).

Another way to fit larger values into a small amount of memory is to take advantage of the unsigned type modifier when storing values which are always non-negative. The unsigned modifier doubles the size of the positive integer which can be stored in the same sized memory location. On a machine with 16 bit ints (e.g., Lattice C on the IBM PC) this means that a 16-bit int can hold values up to 32,767 and an unsigned int can hold values up to 65,535.

There may be opportunities to use some of the ideas from data compaction when trying to reduce the size of an array by changing to a smaller data type.

When the values which will be stored in an array are outside the range for a smaller data type, but the range of values which they span is limited (e.g., all values will be between 1000 and 1120) then by doing some pre-processing before storing the value (e.g., subtracting 1000) and then doing post-processing when the value is retrieved (e.g., adding 1000) a smaller data type (e.g., a char) can be used for the actual storage.

This is a simple tradeoff between time (speed of access) and space (size of the array).

To improve reliability, it is worthwhile to localize (in a single routine) the accesses to an array which contains "biased" information. This will minimize the chance for errors which result from forgetting to do the correct pre- and post-processing.

Another form of compaction can be done when "almost all" of the values fall within the range of a smaller data type. For example, if 95% of the values which will be stored in an array fall between 0 and 10,000, and the other 5% percent may be as large as a million then short integers can be used in the array, if pre- and post-processing is done.

In this case it is possible to use a "special" value (e.g., 32767, the largest portable value for the short data type) in locations where the actual value will not fit in the small data type array. The pre-processing would consist of checking to see if the value would fit within the small data type's storage. If it fits then it is simply stored in the desired location. If it is a value which will not fit, then the special value is stored into the array.

If the special value was stored into the array, then the actual value is then saved in a small secondary structure which has locations large enough to save the correct value. In addition, the index must be stored to tell where the original value belongs.

```
array  [0] |   33    |        |   1   |   | 987,654 |
           |_____|        |_____|   |_____|
       [1] |  32767  |        |  ...  |   |   ...   |
           |_____|        |_____|   |_____|
       [2] |   17    |
           |_____|
           |   ...   |
           |_____|
```

When the array location is accessed, post-processing must be done to check for the special value and to access the secondary structure if necessary.

The secondary structure can be whatever suits the problem best. If the number of exception cases is small then a pair of parallel arrays can be used. The first holds the index (assuming it is only a one dimensional array), and the second holds the actual value. A search of the index array is done to find the position of the saved value.

A variation on this theme can be used when the values are all positive (or negative). Instead of storing the "special value," the negative of the index into a secondary array is stored. This greatly simplifies the secondary structure since no index information needs to be stored in the structure. In addition this can greatly speed up the process of finding the desired value.

Compaction of several values into a single memory location can also be accomplished by using bit-fields in structures. This is discussed in the next section, "Bit Packing."

A few words of caution: The smaller data types do not necessarily mean faster execution. In fact, using variables with char or short types in calculations may cause the extra execution overhead of widening the values to int size before the calculation takes place. This conversion penalty is also possible when variables of float type are used in calculations. The float value is converted to a double before the calculation takes place. As we saw in our timing tables in Chapter 2, this has a significant impact on the calculation speeds of a program. (ANSI C envisions the relaxation of the requirement to widen float to double, so future compilers may be able to handle float more efficiently. Check your manual.)

The techniques which require pre- and post-processing are generally only worthwhile on fairly large arrays. These techniques produce smaller data spaces, but all of the pre- and post-processing requires additional text space. This increase in text space must be considered so that you don't "optimize" yourself into an overall larger program.

7.3 Bit Packing

C allows the programmer fine control over how much memory will be used to hold variables, even beyond the selection of standard types. Bit fields allow the program developer to specify exactly how many bits are to be used to hold a value (from 1 up to the size of an int). This facility, which is only available in structures, allows the encoding of several fields into one word of memory, an obvious savings in space. For an example from Plum [1985], consider a structure that can hold the digits of a time-of-day display in 32 bits:

```
typedef struct time_day
    {
    unsigned h1 : 2;     /* units digit of hours      {0:2} */
    unsigned h2 : 4;     /* tens digit of hours       {0:9} */
    unsigned m1 : 3;     /* units digit of minutes    {0:5} */
    unsigned m2 : 4;     /* tens digit of minutes     {0:9} */
    unsigned s1 : 3;     /* units digit of seconds    {0:5} */
    unsigned s2 : 4;     /* tens digit of seconds     {0:9} */
    unsigned f1 : 4;     /* first digit of fraction   {0:9} */
    unsigned f2 : 4;     /* second digit of fraction  {0:9} */
    unsigned f3 : 4;     /* third digit of fraction   {0:9} */
    } TIME_DAY;          /* 32 bits total */
```

As with the char variables discussed earlier, some care must be used when using values from bit-fields in calculations. The most portable type for bit-fields is unsigned (int); anything else is subject to varying interpretations.

Another potential problem with bit-fields is that there is no guarantee whether the bits will be allocated from right to left or from left to right within the word. This problem would not have any effect when accessing the fields using the standard references, but it could cause problems when trying to align bit-fields to correspond to a hardware layout (e.g., the control word for a port). The documentation for your compiler should specify which direction it uses when allocating bit-fields in a word.

As was discussed in the examples in Section 4.2, the low level C capabilities (AND, OR, and shift) allow the C programmer to simulate these bit packing capabilities with a simple integer type.

There is no clear rule for whether the direct use of bit-fields or the use of the bitwise operators to simulate bit-fields is faster, but both techniques may be used to save data space.

Whether the accessing of bit-fields is competitive with the accessing of normal integers is dependent primarily upon whether the hardware instruction set supports accessing and testing individual bit-fields. Unless bit-field manipulation instructions are available on the target hardware it will not be worthwhile to use bit-fields for variables which do not appear in an array of structures or as part of a structure which appears multiple times (as in a node in a linked list or binary tree).

Our timing studies indicated that the testing and setting of single bits was somewhat faster with explicit bitwise operations than with bit-field operations. We did not find any consistent differences in the extraction and setting of multi-bit bit-fields, as compared with explicit bitwise operations.

7.4 Unions

Another C language feature which can be used to conserve space is a union. Unions allow the same memory to be used to hold different objects (at different times).

The use of unions is particularly valuable in structures which are used to hold many different types of things. This frequently occurs when a structure must hold different information depending on what kind of item (from the class being handled) is being handled.

For example, in a C compiler the information stored with a symbol is much different for the name of an array than for the name of a structure. The straightforward approach would be to allocate a list of fields for every piece of information which is needed in every case. The problem is that this generates a very large structure for each symbol. In addition, for any one symbol most of the fields would never be used because the fields are for symbols of a different type.

C programmers can avoid this enormous waste of space by using a union. This allows the fields which will not be active at the same time to share the same memory locations. In the above example the dimension information for an array may use the same memory locations as would be used by the element list for a structure symbol.

7.5 Array vs Linked Data Structures

In many dynamic data structures a large amount of the space is dedicated to links which connect the pieces together. The cost of links (particularly if they are four-byte pointers) can become the dominant factor in the size of a linked structure.

When a reasonable upper bound can be placed on the size of a structure, it can be more efficient to use a simpler data structure such as array. If the array has fewer elements than that which can be held in an unsigned short (typically two bytes long; 65,535 items) , then all of the "pointers" to other objects in the array can use unsigned short types. Arrays also allow the use of "implicit" links based upon the static properties of the array. These implicit links do not require any storage. For example, the next right node in a tree could always be contained in the next contiguous location in the array.

One technique for storing a series of lists within an array is to designate an end-of-list value and then store each of the items in the list in consecutive locations in the array and end the list with the "end-of-list value". Now the only list overhead is the array index which tells where the list starts and the extra entry at the end of each list (for the end-of-list entry). This approach is used successfully in the UNIX System V C compiler to store the variable-length lists of information related to array dimensions in C programs.

An alternate approach to the "end-of-list marker" is to use a count field for the number of entries at the beginning of each list.

7.6 Dynamic vs Static Allocation

C allows a programmer to dynamically allocate space as required during the execution of a program. This space (which is allocated using a function like `malloc`) is then accessed via pointers. The dynamic structures allow a program to utilize only the space required for a particular execution of the program.

If multiple structures are required during different, non-overlapping portions of a program, dynamic structures give a reliable way of allowing the structures to share the same physical memory.

When the first structure is no longer needed, then the memory is "given back" via a call to `free` (or the equivalent). This memory is then available for the data structures of the next phase.

If the lifetimes of the data structures overlap, then this technique is primarily useful when conditions hold that when one structure is large the other(s) will be small (and vice versa). Consider a program which uses three arrays A, B, and C, each of which holds 500 structures. If we statically allocate all three of the arrays and then, during execution, need to save 501 objects in A, we will run out of space. This overflow will happen even if the space for B and C objects is currently not being used. Dynamic allocation allows a fuller use of the available memory.

If the arrays (or structures) can reach their maximum size at the same time, then the same amount of memory as would be required by statically allocating the maximum size of each array may be required. If this is the case then the dynamic structure may actually be less efficient because it must be accessed indirectly via a pointer. In addition, since many structures are built piece by piece (e.g., a linked list), they may contain links which require additional space.

One drawback to the static allocation of structures is that if additional memory becomes available (e.g., a memory expansion board is put into an IBM PC) the program is unable to take advantage of it to handle larger problems.   This additional space would typically be available if a dynamic memory allocation approach was used.

7.7 Controlling the Growth of the Stack

Reducing the amount of stack space which is used by a program can have a significant impact on the total space requirements for a program.   This is particularly helpful when a recursive function may recurse to a very deep level.

One approach is to use static variables, or allocated storage, instead of local (auto or static) variables for any values which do not need to be unique with each instance of the recursive function.   This also applies to function arguments.

This approach avoids the space for multiple copies of the variable on the stack.   Care must be taken to ensure that there are no name conflicts and that the modularity of the program is not sacrificed when using this approach.   Another possible drawback is that re-entrancy (the ability to re-use the function when servicing an interrupt) is lost when making use of static storage in this way.

Another, more radical, way to reduce stack space is to change an algorithm which uses a recursive approach to one which uses an iterative approach.

The quicksort function shown in Chapter 4 is a good example. The algorithm is elegant, but not practical for very large arrays. Since we are using recursion to handle each of the sub-tables, the worst case can build a stack that is almost equal in depth to the number of array elements.

The following iterative version of the qsort function avoids most of this overhead.

```
qsort(iter):
    /* qsort - sort array a (dimension n) using quicksort
     * based on Bentley, CACM April 84
     * Iterative version; avoids recursion, uses little stack
     * Comments use notation A[i], a (fictitious) array of things
     * that are of size elt_size.
     * Uses static storage, not re-entrant.
     */
    #include "local.h"

    #define STACK_DEPTH (sizeof(size_t) * CHAR_BIT)

    static size_t elt_size = 0;      /* size of one element */
    static int (*cmpfn)() = NULL;    /* the comparison function ptr */
    /* swapfn - swap  elt_size bytes  a <--> b (internal routine)  */
    static void swapfn(a, b)
        register char *a;    /* pointer to one element of A */
        register char *b;    /* pointer to another element of A */
        {
        register size_t i;
        char tmp;

        LOOPDN(i, elt_size)
            {
            SWAP(*a, *b, tmp);
            ++a, ++b;
            }
        }
```

```
/* sort1 - partition one (sub)array, returning p_lastlo */
static char *sort1(p_lo, p_hi)
    char *p_lo;          /* ptr to low element of (sub)array */
    char *p_hi;          /* ptr to high element of (sub)array */
    {
    char *p_mid;
    register char *p_i;          /* pointer to A[i] */
    register char *p_lastlo;     /* pointer to A[lastlo] */

    p_mid = p_lo + ((((p_hi - p_lo) / elt_size) / 2) * elt_size);
    swapfn(p_lo, p_mid);         /* pick the middle element as pivot */
    p_lastlo = p_lo;
    for (p_i = p_lo + elt_size;  p_i <= p_hi; p_i += elt_size)
        {
        if ((*cmpfn)(p_lo, p_i) > 0)
            {
            p_lastlo += elt_size;
            swapfn(p_lastlo, p_i);
            }
        }
    swapfn(p_lo, p_lastlo);
    return (p_lastlo);
    }

/* qsort - the callable entry point */
void qsort(a, n, size, pf)
    data_ptr a;      /* address of array A to be sorted */
    size_t n;        /* number of elements in A */
    size_t size;     /* size of each element */
    int (*pf)();     /* comparison function ptr */
    {
    static char *histack[STACK_DEPTH] = {0};
    static char *lostack[STACK_DEPTH] = {0};
    int istack;              /* index of next free stack cell */
    char *p_lo;              /* ptr to A[lo] */
    char *p_hi;              /* ptr to A[hi] */
    char *p_lastlo;          /* ptr to A[lastlo] */
    char *p_lo1, *p_hi1;     /* partition 1 */
    char *p_lo2, *p_hi2;     /* partition 2 */
    char *tpc;               /* tmp ptr for swaps */

    elt_size = size;
    cmpfn = pf;
    istack = 0;
    p_lo = a;
    p_hi = (char *)a + (n-1) * elt_size;
```

```
          /* loop until no non-trivial partitions remain */
          while (istack != 0 || p_lo < p_hi)
              {
              p_lastlo = sort1(p_lo, p_hi);
              p_lo1 = p_lo;
              p_hi1 = p_lastlo - elt_size;
              p_lo2 = p_lastlo + elt_size;
              p_hi2 = p_hi;
              if (p_hi1 - p_lo1 > p_hi2 - p_lo2)
                  {
                  SWAP(p_lo1, p_lo2, tpc);
                  SWAP(p_hi1, p_hi2, tpc);
                  }
              /* now [p_lo1,p_hi1] is smaller partition */
              if (p_lo1 >= p_hi1)
                  {
                  if (p_lo2 < p_hi2)
                      {
                      /* do next iteration on [p_lo2, p_hi2] */
                      p_lo = p_lo2;
                      p_hi = p_hi2;
                      }
                  else if (istack > 0)
                      {
                      /* take next iteration from stack */
                      --istack;
                      p_hi = histack[istack];
                      p_lo = lostack[istack];
                      }
                  else
                      p_hi = p_lo;     /* done */
                  }
              else
                  {
                  /* push [p_lo2, p_hi2] on stack */
                  histack[istack] = p_hi2;
                  lostack[istack] = p_lo2;
                  ++istack;
                  /* take next iteration from [p_lo1, p_hi1] */
                  p_lo = p_lo1;
                  p_hi = p_hi1;
                  }
              }
          }
```

The repeated function call overhead, as well as the repeated local variables, are eliminated in the second version because an explicit stack is kept by the program. The size of this stack is now proportional to the base-2 log of the number of array elements, since we always save the information on the largest subtable and immediately sort the smaller subtable. For a specific illustration, consider the sorting of a 1000-element array. For the recursive version, there is always some ordering of the data which causes the stack to grow to nearly 1000 frames in depth. Even if each frame took only 20 bytes (for arguments, local variables, and bookkeeping overhead), the function would consume about 20,000 bytes of stack space at the deepest point. The iterative version, on the other hand, has two statically-declared stacks each containing only 16 or 32 pointers.

One penalty that we paid in making the change was that the iterative version is not re-entrant. It stores all its relevant state information in static memory, so it could not be called from an interrupt-level routine.

We did not pay an execution-time penalty for the change to the iterative version. In any quicksort implementation, the execution time is roughly proportional to N log N (where N is the number of array elements, and the base-2 log is conventionally used). We timed the execution of this revised quicksort function, using test cases of randomly-generated arrays of 100, 1000, and 10,000 ints, and obtained the following times:

		8088/PC Lattice	PDP-11/23 WSL	MC68000 V/68	VAX-11/780 UNIX V
100:	time (msec)	187.	267.	83.	50.
1000:	time (msec)	2827.	3883.	1317.	850.
10000:	time (msec)	46427.	44383.	17333.	11267.
100:	time / N log N	281.	401.	125.	75.3
1000:	time / N log N	283.	389.	132.	85.3
10000:	time / N log N	349.	334.	130.	84.8

In all cases, these were actually less than the times for the recursive version. The program which generated the timings is reproduced in the appendix [7-1].

7.8 Using a Function to Represent Data

One technique which is not widely used but which can have significant savings in some specialized contexts is to save a recipe for regenerating information rather than saving the information itself.

For example, if a screen image is generated using a random number and a selected function, it would be more compact to save the random number seed and a pointer to the selected function rather than all of the data points on the screen.

CHAPTER 8: TRANSLATION INTO C

As we have noted in earlier chapters, it is very important to use a good algorithm. The process of using efficient C techniques to improve a poor algorithm will usually meet with limited success, at best.

This fact leads us to look for good algorithms in the literature. Unfortunately, if we find a good algorithm it frequently has been written in a language other than C. We are, therefore, faced with the prospect of translating the program into C.

We do not gain many of the advantages of C if we do a straightforward statement by statement translation from another language into C without regard for the features and strengths of C. We will not be effective if we write FORTRAN- or Pascal-style programs in C.

In this chapter we will look at the process of recoding programs from other languages into C.

8.1 The detab Program

As our first example we will look at a Pascal program named detab which converts tabs to an equivalent number of blanks. This program is taken from the excellent reference *Software Tools in Pascal* [Kernighan and Plauger, 1981]. Here is their description of detab:

> detab copies its input to its output, expanding horizontal tabs to blanks along the way, so that the output is visually the same as the input, but contains no tab characters. Tab stops are assumed to be set every four columns (i.e., 1, 5, 9, ...), so

that each tab character is replaced by from one to four blanks.

The Pascal version of the program follows.

```
detab.p:
    { detab -- convert tabs to equivalent number of blanks }
    procedure detab;
    const
        MAXLINE = 1000;      { or whatever }
    type
        tabtype = array [1..MAXLINE] of boolean;
    var
        c : character;
        col : integer;
        tabstops : tabtype;
    #include "tabpos.p"
    #include "settabs.p"
    begin
        settabs(tabstops);   {set initial tap stops }
        col := 1;
        while (getc(c) <> ENDFILE) do
            if (c = TAB) then
                repeat
                    putc(BLANK);
                    col := col + 1
                until (tabpos(col, tabstops))
            else if (c = NEWLINE) then begin
                putc(NEWLINE);
                col := 1
            end
            else begin
                putc(c);
                col := col + 1
            end
    end;
```

where `tabpos` and `settabs` are as follows:

```
tabpos.p:
    {tabpos -- return true if col is a tab stop }
    function tabpos (col : integer; var tabstops : tabtype)
        : boolean;
    begin
        if (col > MAXLINE) then
            tabpos := true
        else
            tabpos := tabstops[col]
    end;
```

```
settabs.p:
    { settabs -- set initial tab stops }
    procedure settabs (var tabstops : tabtype);
    const
        TABSPACE = 4;    {4 spaces per tab }
    var
        i : integer;
    begin
        for i := 1 to MAXLINE do
            tabstops[i] := (i mod TABSPACE = 1)
    end;
```

Our first pass at translating these three routines will be a straight-forward change which concentrates primarily on changing the Pascal syntax into the correct corresponding C syntax. The following code shows the results of this translation into C.

detab(#1):
```
    /* detab - convert tabs to equivalent number of blanks */
    #include "local.h"
    #define MAXLINE 1000

    typedef tbool tabtype[MAXLINE+1];

    tbool tabpos();
    void settabs();

    main()
        {
        metachar c;
        int col;
        tabtype tabstops;

        settabs(tabstops);
        col = 1;
        while ((c = getchar()) != EOF)
            if (c == '\t')
                do
                    {
                    putchar(' ');
                    col = col + 1;
                    }
                while (!tabpos(col, tabstops));
            else if (c == '\n')
                {
                putchar('\n');
                col = 1;
                }
            else
                {
                putchar(c);
                col = col + 1;
                }
        } /* end of detab */

    /* tabpos -- return true if col is a tab stop */
    tbool tabpos(col, tabstops)
        int col;
        tabtype tabstops;
        {
        if (col > MAXLINE)
            return (TRUE);
        else
            return(tabstops[col]);
        } /* end of tabpos */
```

```
/* settabs -- set initial tab stops */
#define TABSPACE 4
void settabs(tabstops)
    tabtype tabstops;
    {
    int i;

    for (i = 1; i <= MAXLINE; ++i)
        tabstops[i] = (i % TABSPACE == 1);
    } /* end of settabs */
```

A couple of comments on this translation may be useful. We could have translated the tabstops array into a structure with an array of packed bits. This would have been considerably more compact (saving 875 bytes of data space), but it is significantly slower (as discussed in Section 4.2).

In this example, we selected the faster, larger tbool (char) array because of a bias for speed and because the tbool array references more closely matched the way the Pascal boolean array was referenced.

When we discuss the optimization of the detab program, it is important to consider that this algorithm might be found in two very different contexts: (1) It might be the preliminary embodiment of a time-critical terminal handler for an operating system or other low-level environment; or (2) it might be the first version of a utility program, to be run as one of many commands on a time-sharing system. Our criteria for optimization will be quite different in these contexts. The first context is one where both time and space will be of extreme importance. In the second context, the I/O time is likely to exceed the program logic time, and the addition of new features is most likely. In particular, user-settable tab positions will almost certainly be added at some point. In the first context, if we know that user-settable tabs will never be added to the design, the tabtype array can be dropped in favor of a simpler calculation.

We will now step through the process of making the program into a C-style program which uses some of the efficiency techniques which have been discussed in this book.

As a first step the col = col + 1 expressions are changed to ++col. Next, the variables col and c are made into register variables. As was noted in both the chapters on improving space and time the effective use of register variables can significantly improve the performance of a program.

Next the tabpos function is replaced by a macro. The major reason for this improvement is that it eliminates the function call in the loop which outputs blanks for the tabs.

Finally, a fairly specialized modification is made to the settabs function. This function spends a large portion of its time doing the

    i % TABSPACE

operation. As we saw in Chapter 2, the modulus (remainder) operation is very expensive, between 5 and 50 times more time-consuming than a bitwise AND. The change represents a shift away from user-settable tabs; the default four-space tabs could only be changed to eight-space tabs, or some other power of two. The bitwise AND is embodied in a macro named MOD4, so that the modification restriction is clearer.

The following program reflects all of the changes which have been discussed in the preceding paragraphs.

```
detab(#2):
    /* detab - convert tabs to equivalent number of blanks */
    #include "local.h"
    #define MAXLINE 1000

    typedef tbool tabtype[MAXLINE+1];
    /* tabpos -- return true if col is a tab stop */
    #define tabpos(col, tabstops) \
        (col > MAXLINE ? TRUE : tabstops[col])
    #define MOD4(n) (n & 0x3)

    void settabs();

    main()
        {
        register int c;
        register int col;
        tabtype tabstops;

        settabs(tabstops);
        col = 1;
        while ((c = getchar()) != EOF)
            if (c == '\t')
                do
                    {
                    putchar(' ');
                    ++col;
                    }
                while (!tabpos(col, tabstops));
            else if (c == '\n')
                {
                putchar('\n');
                col = 1;
                }
            else
                {
                putchar(c);
                ++col;
                }
        } /* end of detab */

    /* settabs -- set initial tab stops */
    void settabs(tabstops)
        tabtype tabstops;
        {
        int i;

        for (i = 1; i <= MAXLINE; ++i)
            tabstops[i] = (MOD4(i) == 1);
        } /* end of settabs */
```

We have taken a "good" program and modified it by applying a series of fairly simple code improvements. Whether one considers the changes worthwhile depends upon one's context, as we mentioned earlier. Timing the PDP-11 Idris version with the time command gives the following results: For a 1000-byte input file (a C source program), the first version takes 0.56 seconds user time and 6.43 seconds system time. The second version takes 0.42 seconds user time and 6.42 seconds system time. If the algorithm is intended for a time-critical context like a terminal handler, the 25% decrease in the function's own time requirement may be significant. If the program is intended as a utility command, the time spent performing I/O far outweighs the internal processing time, and any marginal performance improvement cannot outweigh the loss of flexibility.

8.2 The ctoi Function

Next, let us look at another function from *Software Tools in Pascal*. The function ctoi converts a string of characters to an integer. It also updates the index in the string to indicate the next character following the end of the number. The following is the original Pascal version of the program.

```
ctoi.p:
    { ctoi -- convert string at s[i] to integer, increment i }
    function ctoi (var s : string; var i : integer) : integer;
    var
        n, sign : integer;
    begin
        while (s[i] = BLANK) or (s[i] = TAB) do
            i := i + 1;
        if (s[i] = MINUS) then
            sign := -1
        else
            sign := 1;
        if (s[i] = PLUS) or (s[i] = MINUS) then
            i = i + 1;
        n := 0;
        while (isdigit(s[i])) do begin
            n := 10 * n + s[i] - ord('0');
            i := i + 1
        end;
        ctoi := sign * n
    end;

    { isdigit -- true if c is a digit }
    function isdigit (c : character) : boolean;
    begin
        isdigit := c in [ord('0')..ord('9')]
    end;
```

The first pass at recoding this function in C is, as before, a direct translation from Pascal syntax to C syntax. The following code shows the translation:

```
ctoi(#1):
    /* ctoi -- convert string at s[i] to integer, increment i */
    #include <ctype.h>
    int ctoi(s, pi)
        char s[];
        int *pi;
        {
        int n;
        int sign;
        int i = *pi;

        while (s[i] == ' ' || s[i] == '\t')
            i = i + 1;
        if (s[i] == '-')
            sign = -1;
        else
            sign = 1;
        if (s[i] == '+' || s[i] == '-')
            i = i + 1;
        n = 0;
        while (isdigit(s[i]))
            {
            n = 10 * n + s[i] - '0';
            i = i + 1;
            }
        *pi = i;
        return (sign * n);
        }
```

The improvements begin by applying the same kind of code changes as were discussed in the previous example. The increment operator is used where appropriate. The key variables, s, i, n, and sign are made register variables.

The following code shows how the function looks after applying the changes.

```
ctoi(#2):
    /* ctoi -- convert string at s[i] to integer, increment i */
    #include <ctype.h>
    int ctoi(s, pi)
        register char s[];
        int *pi;
        {
        register int n;
        int sign;
        register int i = *pi;

        while (s[i] == ' ' || s[i] == '\t')
            ++i;
        if (s[i] == '-')
            sign = -1;
        else
            sign = 1;
        if (s[i] == '+' || s[i] == '-')
            ++i;
        n = 0;
        while (isdigit(s[i]))
            {
            n = 10 * n + s[i] - '0';
            ++i;
            }
        *pi = i;
        return (sign * n);
        }
```

The ctoi function makes extensive use of subscripts and is therefore a prime candidate for converting the subscripts into pointer references. The following code shows the conversion:

```
ctoi(#3):
    /* ctoi -- convert string at s[i] to integer, increment i */
    #include <ctype.h>
    int ctoi(s, pi)
        char s[];
        int *pi;
        {
        register int n;
        int sign;
        register char *cp = s + *pi;

        while (*cp == ' ' || *cp == '\t')
            ++cp;
        if (*cp == '-')
            sign = -1;
        else
            sign = 1;
        if (*cp == '+' || *cp == '-')
            ++cp;
        n = 0;
        while (isdigit(*cp))
            {
            n = 10 * n + *cp - '0';
            ++cp;
            }
        *pi = cp - s;
        return (sign * n);
        }
```

All of the subscripted array references have been changed to use pointer indirection.

We timed the three versions in the PDP-11 (Idris) environment, using the string "12345 " as the input. Version 1 took 744 microseconds, version 2 took 579 microseconds, and version 3 took 544 microseconds, for a total improvement of 27%.

8.3 Summary

The key to the effective translation of C from other languages is to first look for the commonality so that an accurate first translation can be done. It is useful to concentrate on the similarities, with a watchful eye for similar but not quite the same features. For example, the concluding test of Pascal's repeat-until is just the opposite of the test used in C's do-while.

After the initial translation is done, we can concentrate on the features and capabilities which are available in C but which are not available in the original language. Using these features as a check list we review the program to see where the unique C features could be applied to some advantage. We will usually be looking for opportunities to use special C features like the increment and decrement operators (++ and --), register, pointers, and the bitwise operators.

We should also watch for opportunities to use C's rich library of functions. In fact, our second example, ctoi is much like the atoi function already in the library, and of course we made use of the generally-efficient isdigit. We could use these library functions instead of going through the time and effort of porting and improving the function from another language.

The process of translating code from another language is very similar to the general process of writing efficient C code. It is part science and part art. It is a process which requires an understanding of the goals and requirements of the program as well as the techniques that are at the programmer's disposal. It takes work and understanding and, if the job is done well, it will result in a high quality, efficient program.

APPENDIX

[1-1] The "Average C Operator"

We chose not to take a simple average of all the times reported for each operator tested in our timing suite. The extreme cases would skew the average so much as to be unuseable. Instead, we performed a rather crude "cluster analysis." By an iterative process, we partitioned each set of measurements into low extremes, a middle group, and high extremes. The times in the middle group were no less than one-third of, and no more than three times, the arithmetic average of the middle group. This was the "average operator" time that was reported.

[2-1] The Assumptions of the Timing Method

We wish to acknowledge that our timing method assumes in various ways that extreme optimizations are not being performed upon the timed code. Stripped of all the complications, we are executing a piece of code some number of times (as many as ten million), and assuming that the resulting time (after subtracting an amount for the timing "harness") can simply be divided by the number of iterations. This assumes that repetitive execution times are additive, and that the code sample is meaningfully repeatable.

In the terminology of the emerging ANSI C standard, we are assuming that the data objects are "volatile" — that is, that the compiler will faithfully compute the million iterations, or whatever was specified. An extreme optimizer might notice that the million iterations were to no purpose, and repeat the sample only once. Alternatively, some but not all of the code in the timed loop might be evaluated prior to the loop.

We did not detect any of these extreme optimizations being done in the compilers that we used. Such optimizations would, of course, make the compiler unsuitable for writing device drivers, unless there were some special way to tell the compiler not to perform the optimizations. In the emerging ANSI usage, we would add the keyword volatile to the declaration of all variables for which we wanted to guarantee literal evaluation of all expressions.

Another assumption made is that the number of code bytes required for a compound statement can be determined if we know the address of the start of the statement and the address of the end of the statement. This was true for all the simple cases that we measured, but a compiler such as Whitesmiths which rearranges blocks of code for jump optimization can invalidate this assumption when the code sample being measured has loops in it.

[2-2] The cputim Function

In the environment of UNIX systems (and look-alikes), the implementation of cputim is simple but coarse. We use the accumulated process execution times that are reported by the times system call. Upon return from times, we receive the accumulated user time and system time for the timed process and for its children. (None of our timed programs spawned any others, but the timing method would include them if it did.) All these times are reported in line-clock ticks (60 Hz in the Americas, 50 Hz in Europe), as specified by CLOCK_TICKS_PER_SECOND in cputim.h. The function returns the difference in total ticks between the current invocation and the previous invocation.

On Whitesmiths' Idris 2.3, and other kernels whose system calls resemble UNIX Edition 6, the third and fourth members of a TBUF are unsigned short integers. (The stated declarations should really be unsigned long, but the distinction is purely academic for reasonable intervals of time.)

Here are the contents of the header cputim.h and the function cputim for the UNIX environments:

```
unix/cputim.h:
   /* cputim.h  */
   #ifndef TIME_H
   #define TIME_H
   #define CLOCK_TICKS_PER_SECOND 60
   typedef long cputim_t;
   extern cputim_t cputim();
   #endif
```

```
unix/cputim:
    /* cputim - UNIX version
     */


    #define UTIME (tbufb.ut - tbufa.ut + tbufb.cut - tbufa.cut)
    #define STIME (tbufb.st - tbufa.st + tbufb.cst - tbufa.cst)

    typedef struct tbuf {    /* UNIX V7 ff    */
        long ut, st;
        long cut, cst;
    } TBUF;

    long times();

    /*
     * cputim - return (in ticks) CPU time since last call
     */
    long cputim()
    {
        long ret;
        long ut1, st1, i;
        static TBUF tbufa = {0, 0, 0, 0};
        static TBUF tbufb = {0, 0, 0, 0};

        times(&tbufb);
        ut1 = UTIME;
        st1 = STIME;
        ret = (ut1 + st1);

        tbufa = tbufb;
        return (ret);
    }
```

In the MS-DOS environment, we took quite a different approach. The clock chip of the PC environment provides a timer with a 1.193182 MHz rate, but the cputim function becomes much more elaborate. The assembler routine ntim_int.asm produces three unsigned (short) integers which constitute a 48-bit time reading. The C function cputim starts up the timer channel zero in "mode two." (WARNING: If the code being timed makes assumptions about timer channel zero, there may be conflicts!) To oversimplify for a moment, cputim simply subtracts the low-order 32 bits of the old time reading from the low-order 32 bits of the new time reading, to produce a 32-bit time difference that represents the time between successive invocations.

Here are the complications: The initial reading was observed to be unduly variable, so the first call to cputim soaks up some time and then calls itself again before returning. The second complication is that the middle 16 bits of the time reading constitute the "BIOS clock" maintained by DOS, and each time this clock increments, DOS takes about

136 clock ticks to service the interrupt. This overhead needs to be subtracted from the reported time whenever the BIOS clock has ticked since the last call. The third complication is that the time required to execute the cputim function itself is quite large, relative to the speed of the clock. This overhead (about 453 ticks) needs to be subtracted each time. The final complication is that we attempted to ensure that the function takes the same amount of time to execute, no matter which flow path is followed; two "junk" variables are used to balance the timings.

For applications that want to call cputim repeatedly and then add up the successive intervals to match true elapsed time, the cumulative overhead needs to be made available. The global variable clockfuzz gives a cumulative total of the number of overhead ticks which have been subtracted from cputim readings.

We would like to acknowledge Christopher Skelly for the implementation of cputim and ntim_int.asm in the PC environment. Important techniques came from Smith and Pucket [1984]. We disregarded one of their suggestions, however. In the ntim_int.asm function, there is a critical region in which interrupts should be disabled. We commented out the disable and enable instructions, not being sure about any system-wide implications to disabling interrupts. (See the listing.) There is a somewhat more complicated way to handle a critical region like this without disabling interrupts: Sample the high-order timer first, then the low-order, then the high-order again. If the low-order is in its lower half-range, use the second high-order sample. Otherwise, use the first high-order sample.

The timing suites executed marvelously quickly in the PC environment; we used a criterion of 1000 microseconds in excess of the harness time, and achieved total repeatability of results. One last note of caution: when we were timing functions that involved I/O, we found it useful to increase the criterion to the same 200/60 seconds used in the other environments. Otherwise, we were only timing the first invocation of the function being timed, which takes extra time to fill the first buffer, etc.

Here are the header and functions used in the MS-DOS 8088 environment:

dos/cputim.h:

```
/* cputim.h  */
#ifndef TIME_H
#define TIME_H
#define CLOCK_TICKS_PER_SECOND 1193182
typedef long cputim_t;
extern cputim_t cputim();
#endif
```

dos/cputim:

```
/*
 *    cputim.c            Christopher Skelly
 *
 *        Returns a long time containing the number of clock
 *        ticks since the last call of cputim. Returns zero on
 *        the first call. Clock assumes a 1.193182e+6 standard
 *        PC clockrate, and sets 8253 timer channel zero to
 *        operate in mode two on the first call.
 *
 */
#include <stdio.h>

#define COUNTDOWN    65535
#define BIOSOVHD     136        /* ticks per bios-tick overhead */
#define OVHD         453        /* overhead for fn execution */

long clockfuzz = 0;             /* cumulative time correction */

/* cputim - return time (in ticks) since last call */
long cputim()
    {
    extern ntim_int();          /* 8086 routine to load the time struct   */

    unsigned latch_dif;         /* timer latch difference since last call */
    unsigned cnt_dif;           /* BIOS TIMER_LOW difference (corrected)  */
    unsigned ovhd = OVHD;       /* overhead from bios-tick + fn-exec */
    unsigned junk = ~0;         /* used so all calls take same time */
    unsigned junk2 = ~0;        /* used so all calls take same time */
    static int first = 1;       /* flag for first call        */

    static struct t
        {
        unsigned latch;
        unsigned tlow;
        unsigned thigh;
        } time = {0}, oldtime = {0};
```

```
/* if first entry, initialize the clock chip */
if (first)  /* first time through */
    {
    /* set the 8253 timer chip:
     * channel 0, mode 2, write bytes */
    outp(67, 52);    /* 00110100b */
    outp(64, 0);
    outp(64, 0);

    first = 0;

    for (junk = 64000; junk < 65000; ++junk)
        ;           /* soak up some time */
    cputim();    /* make first result more reliable */
    }

ntim_int(&time);     /* 8086 routine */

cnt_dif = time.tlow - oldtime.tlow;

if (time.latch < oldtime.latch)
    --cnt_dif, ovhd += BIOSOVHD;     /* "borrow" */
else
    --junk, junk2 += BIOSOVHD;

latch_dif = time.latch - oldtime.latch;

oldtime.latch = time.latch;
oldtime.thigh = time.thigh;
oldtime.tlow  = time.tlow;

clockfuzz += cnt_dif * BIOSOVHD + ovhd;

return ((long)cnt_dif * (COUNTDOWN-BIOSOVHD) + latch_dif - ovhd);
    }
```

```
dos/ntimint.asm:
    ;NTIM_INT - ACCESS 8253 CLOCK - CHRISTOPHER SKELLY
    PGROUP  GROUP   PROG              ; Standard heading
    PROG    SEGMENT BYTE PUBLIC 'PROG'
            ASSUME CS:PGROUP
    REG     STRUC
    AXR     DW      ?
    TLO     DW      ?
    THI     DW      ?
    REG     ENDS
    BIOS_DATA_SEG   EQU     40H
    BIOS_DATA               SEGMENT AT 40H
                    ORG     6CH
    TIMER_LOW       DW      ?
    TIMER_HIGH      DW      ?
    BIOS_DATA       ENDS
    TIMER_0         EQU     40H
    TIMER_CTL       EQU     43H
    TIMER_0_LATCH   EQU     00H
    ;
            PUBLIC  NTIM_INT
    NTIM_INT        PROC    NEAR
            PUSH    BP
            MOV     BP, SP
            MOV     SI, [BP + 4]
            PUSH    DS              ;save data segment
            MOV     AX,  BIOS_DATA_SEG
            MOV     DS, AX
            ASSUME  DS:BIOS_DATA
            MOV     AL, TIMER_0_LATCH
        ;CLI
            OUT     TIMER_CTL, AL
            MOV     BX, TIMER_LOW
            MOV     CX, TIMER_HIGH
            IN      AL, TIMER_0
            MOV     AH, AL
            NOP
            IN      AL, TIMER_0
        ;STI
            XCHG    AH, AL
            NEG     AX
            POP     DS
            MOV     [SI].AXR,  AX
            MOV     [SI].TLO, BX
            MOV     [SI].THI, CX
            POP     BP
            RET
    NTIM_INT ENDP
    PROG    ENDS
            END
```

[2-3] The Timing Suite

The next subsection will describe the detailed workings of the timing suite. If you are interested only in running the suite, and your environment is close enough to ours that you can just copy the functions involved, just skim the details until you reach the installation instructions.

Implementation of the Timing Suite

The suite used to prepare our timings consists of a number of headers and functions. We described the cputim function in the previous note. Next we want to describe the other environment-dependent function, returnp, which tells where *its* caller was called from. In other words, a function calls returnp to find out what (text space) address it will return to. In the VAX environment, it was necessary to pass the address of the first local variable of the function that calls returnp. In the other environments, it was necessary to pass the address of the first argument of the function. The function returnp is trivially simple; it returns the int that it finds at an environment-dependent offset from the address that it is passed. This assumes that text space addresses have the same internal representation as int, which is true in all our sampled environments but hardly universally true.

To be sure, we are going beyond anything that is guaranteed in portable C, when we make an integer out of a text space address. Having acknowledged that, here is the listing of returnp, which #include's an environment-dependent header named config.h:

```
returnp:
    /* returnp - reveal the return pointer of my calling function */
    #include "config.h"
    int returnp(pa)
        int *pa;
        {
        return (pa[RETOFFSET]);
        }
```

Among other things, the config.h header specifies whether the "frame anchor" is the first argument or the first automatic variable, and also specifies the relative offset of the return address. Here are the relevant specifications for our four environments:

	8088/PC Lattice	PDP-11/23 WSL	MC68000 UNIX V	VAX-11/780 UNIX V
FR_ANCHOR	arg1	arg1	arg1	var1
RETOFFSET	-1	-1	-1	5

Besides these two environment parameters, the header config.h provided appropriate typedefs for ushort (unsigned short, or the equivalent), utiny (unsigned char, or equivalent), ulong (unsigned long, or just long if necessary), and void (if the compiler did not already know it as a keyword). Also specified were MINSAM (the minimum number of microseconds required above the harness overhead), NTRY (the maximum number of code excerpts per source file), and JUNKFILE (the name of a file for writing junk output). Here are the four implementations of config.h:

```
dos/config.h:
    /* config.h - configuration data for each environment
    *       This file should either be customized to the intended
    *       compiler/machine environment, or parameterized via -D flags
    *       on the compile step:
    *       -D UTINY     if compiler supports unsigned char
    *       -D USHORT    if compiler supports unsigned short
    *       -D ULONG     if compiler supports unsigned LONG
    *       -D VOID      if compiler supports void
    */
    /* no UTINY - Lattice PC 2.10 compiler */
    /* no USHORT - Lattice PC 2.10 compiler */
    /* no ULONG - Lattice PC 2.10 compiler */
    /* no VOID - Lattice PC 2.10 compiler */
    #ifdef USHORT
    typedef unsigned short ushort;
    #else
    typedef unsigned ushort;      /* assumes short == int */
    #endif
    #ifdef UTINY
    typedef unsigned char utiny;
    #endif
    #ifdef ULONG
    typedef unsigned long ulong;
    #endif
    #ifndef VOID
    #define void int
    #endif
    #define MINSAM 1000     /* minimum timing sample (usec) */
    #define NTRY 100        /* maximum no of code excerpts per file */
    #define FR_ANCHOR arg1  /* what is the "frame anchor": arg1 or var1 */
    #define RETOFFSET (-1)  /* offset of return pointer
                               relative to frame anchor */
    #define JUNKFILE "c:junkfile"
```

```
idris/config.h:
    /* config.h - configuration data for each environment
     *      This file should either be customized to the intended
     *      compiler/machine environment, or parameterized via -D flags
     *      on the compile step:
     *      -D USHORT   if compiler supports unsigned short
     *      -D UTINY    if compiler supports unsigned char
     *      -D VOID     if compiler supports void
     *      -D ULONG    if compiler supports unsigned LONG
     */
    #define UTINY    /* Idris 11 2.3 WSL */
    #define USHORT   /* Idris 11 2.3 WSL */
    #define ULONG    /* Idris 11 2.3 WSL */
    /* no VOID Idris 11 2.3 WSL */
    #ifdef USHORT
    typedef unsigned short ushort;
    #else
    typedef unsigned ushort;      /* assumes short == int */
    #endif
    #ifdef UTINY
    typedef unsigned char utiny;
    #endif
    #ifdef ULONG
    typedef unsigned long ulong;
    #endif
    #ifndef VOID
    #define void int
    #endif
    #define MINSAM 2e6      /* minimum timing sample (usec) */
    #define NTRY 100        /* maximum no of code excerpts per file */
    #define FR_ANCHOR arg1  /* what is the "frame anchor": arg1 or var1 */
    #define RETOFFSET (-1)  /* offset of return pointer
                               relative to frame anchor */

    #define JUNKFILE "/dev/null"

    /* circumvent c 2.3 bug - no ULONG on right-shift */
    #ifdef DRSH
    #undef ULONG
    #endif
```

```
68k/config.h:
    /* config.h - configuration data for each environment
     *       This file should either be customized to the intended
     *       compiler/machine environment, or parameterized via -D flags
     *       on the compile step:
     *       -D USHORT    if compiler supports unsigned short
     *       -D UTINY     if compiler supports unsigned char
     *       -D VOID      if compiler supports void
     *       -D ULONG     if compiler supports unsigned LONG
     */
    #define UTINY    /* UNIX System 3 ff */
    #define USHORT   /* UNIX System 3 ff */
    #define ULONG    /* UNIX System 3 ff */
    #define VOID     /* UNIX System 3 ff */
    #ifdef USHORT
    typedef unsigned short ushort;
    #else
    typedef unsigned ushort;     /* assumes short == int */
    #endif
    #ifdef UTINY
    typedef unsigned char utiny;
    #endif
    #ifdef ULONG
    typedef unsigned long ulong;
    #endif
    #ifndef VOID
    #define void int
    #endif
    #define MINSAM 2e6      /* minimum timing sample (usec) */
    #define NTRY 100        /* maximum no of code excerpts per file */
    #define FR_ANCHOR arg1  /* what is the "frame anchor": arg1 or var1 */
    #define RETOFFSET (-1)  /* offset of return pointer
                               relative to frame anchor */
    #define JUNKFILE "/dev/null"
```

```
vax/config.h:
    /* config.h - configuration data for each environment
     *      This file should either be customized to the intended
     *      compiler/machine environment, or parameterized via -D flags
     *      on the compile step:
     *        -D USHORT    if compiler supports unsigned short
     *        -D UTINY     if compiler supports unsigned char
     *        -D VOID      if compiler supports void
     *        -D ULONG     if compiler supports unsigned LONG
     */
    #define UTINY    /* UNIX System 3 ff */
    #define USHORT   /* UNIX System 3 ff */
    #define ULONG    /* UNIX System 3 ff */
    #define VOID     /* UNIX System 3 ff */
    #ifdef USHORT
    typedef unsigned short ushort;
    #else
    typedef unsigned ushort;      /* assumes short == int */
    #endif
    #ifdef UTINY
    typedef unsigned char utiny;
    #endif
    #ifdef ULONG
    typedef unsigned long ulong;
    #endif
    #ifndef VOID
    #define void int
    #endif
    #define MINSAM 2e6      /* minimum timing sample (usec) */
    #define NTRY 100        /* maximum no of code excerpts per file */
    #define FR_ANCHOR var1  /* what is the "frame anchor": arg1 or var1 */
                            /* VAX UNIX !!! */
    #define RETOFFSET (5)   /* offset of return pointer
                               relative to frame anchor */
    #define JUNKFILE "/dev/null"
```

At the heart of the timing suite are two functions, begintim and endtim. The begintim function is called each time a code sample is about to be timed. It saves some information about the sample, such as a character-string description of the sample, and calls returnp to learn the (program-counter) location of the start of the sample. Its last action is to call cputim to mark the start of execution. The endtim function calls cputim to get the elapsed CPU time, and saves it in an array location associated with this sample. It also calls returnp, to learn the location of the end of the sample. There is one other function involved: report prints the final tabulation of the results. We will discuss some of the complications after the listings of the functions.

```
begint.c:
    /* TIMING FUNCTIONS: BEGINTIM, ENDTIM, REPORT
     */
    #include <stdio.h>
    #include "cputim.h"
    #include "config.h"

    #define MINTYPE 1           /* smallest value of t_type except SKIP */
    #define MAXTYPE 3           /* largest value of t_type */
    #define SKIP 0              /* skip this excerpt */
    #define SKIPTIME -999.99    /* time value for skipped sample */

    extern int *returnp();

    char *t_s = "";             /* descriptive string for this trial */
    long t_reps = 0;            /* number of repetitions this iteration */
    double t_minsam = MINSAM;   /* desired minimum sample */
    double t_sample[NTRY] = {0};/* array of samples */
    short t_try = 0;            /* which trial number is being done next */
    short t_type = 0;           /* selection of timing method */
    char *t_title[NTRY] = {0};  /* array of descriptions for printout */
    short t_size[NTRY] = {0};   /* array of code sizes in bytes */
    double t_ctime[NTRY] = {0}; /* array of actual times */

    int calibrun = 0;           /* is this a calibration run? */

    static double t1 = 0;       /* time needed to run one full sample (usec) */
    static short thistry = -1;  /* try last done by begintim */
    static int *p1 = NULL;      /* return address for the call to begintim */
    static int *p2 = NULL;      /* return address for the call to endtim */

#define PARMS struct parms
PARMS
    {
    double time;
    unsigned space;
    };
PARMS testparms[3] = {0};       /* harness parms for stmt, reg-asst, dbl-asst */
```

```
/* BEGINTIM - START TIMING FOR ONE TRY */
begintim(arg1)
    int arg1;
    {
    int var1;              /* first auto variable */
    int *pa = &FR_ANCHOR;        /* pointer to "frame anchor" */
    static short first = 1; /* first time */
    static long i = 0;      /* counter for timing loop */
    FILE *fpin;             /* file for reading testparms */
    if (t_try >= NTRY)
        {
        printf("reached maximum # of tries; ignored '%s'\n", t_s);
        exit(1);
        }
    t_title[t_try] = t_s;
    if (t_type == SKIP)
        {
        t_size[t_try] = 0;
        t_ctime[t_try] = SKIPTIME;
        return;
        }
    p1 = returnp(pa);
    thistry = t_try;
    if (first && !calibrun)
        {
        first = 0;
        fpin = fopen("parms.dat", "r");
        if (fpin == NULL)
            error("can't open parms.dat;",
                "Run  calib >parms.dat  to create parms.dat");
        while (getc(fpin) != '\n')
            ;
        for (i = 0; i <= 2; ++i)
            {
            if (2 > fscanf(fpin, "%*22c %d %lf",
                &testparms[i].space, &testparms[i].time))
                error("bad data in", "parms.dat");
            while (getc(fpin) != '\n')
                ;
            }
        fclose(fpin);
        }
    cputim();
    }
```

```
/* ENDTIM - COMPUTE TIMES FOR ONE TRIAL */
endtim(arg1)
    int arg1;
    {
    int var1;                /* first auto variable */
    int *pa = &FR_ANCHOR;    /* pointer to "frame anchor" */

    t1 = cputim() / ((double)CLOCK_TICKS_PER_SECOND/1e6);
    if (thistry != t_try)
        return;
    p2 = returnp(pa);
    if (t_type < MINTYPE || MAXTYPE < t_type)
        {
        fprintf(stderr, "wrong t_type: %d; t_try=%d\n", t_type, t_try);
        t_size[t_try] = 0;
        t_ctime[t_try] = SKIPTIME;
        }
    else
        {
        t_size[t_try] = (char *)p2 - (char *)p1 - testparms[t_type-1].space;
        t_ctime[t_try] = t1 / (double)t_reps - testparms[t_type-1].time;
        }
    t_sample[t_try] = t_ctime[t_try] * t_reps;
    }

/* REPORT - PRINT TIMES */
report()
    {
    char *fround(); /* function to round output values */
    short i;        /* counter for printout loop */

    printf("%-20s  %6s  %12s\n",
        "Code sample", "Size", "Time (usec)");
    for (i = 0; i < t_try; i++)
        {
        if (t_ctime[i] == SKIPTIME)
            printf("%-20.20s  %6s  %12s\n", t_title[i], "-", "-");
        else
            {
            if (t_ctime[i] < 0.)
                t_ctime[i] = 0.;
            printf("%-20.20s  %6d  %12s\n",
                t_title[i], t_size[i],
                fround(t_ctime[i], 3, 3));
            }
        }
    }
```

Now for some of the refinements. There are three types of harness used. One assigns an expression result to a (register) variable, one
assigns a result to a double variable, and one makes no assignment (for
timing C statements, as opposed to C expressions). A "dummy" harness
is also provided, to hold a place in the output table for operators which

are invalid for a particular type (such as the "address" operator for register data). Before begintim is called, the timing software records the harness type in the variable t_type. The endtim function uses the t_type value to subtract the number of code bytes in the harness and the number of microseconds required for the harness loop and the extra assignment operation.

The end result of all this work is to record, for each sample, the number of microseconds taken by each iteration of the timed sample and the total number of microseconds achieved in excess of the harness time.

The top-level control of a timing run is provided by a header named timer1.h. It provides four macros which generate the actual timing loop; they are invoked in the sample source file like this:

```
#include "timer1.h"

DO_IEXPR(comment)    integer expression   OO;

DO_FEXPR(comment)    floating expression   OO;

DO_STMT(comment)     statement             OO;

DO_SKIP(comment)     statement             OO;
char *comment;
```

DO_SKIP just reserves a space in the table for an operation which is not being timed. The other macros save the comment string and the appropriate type of harness in external variables accessible to begintim and endtim. The macros then test whether this code sample has achieved a sufficient number of microseconds in excess of the harness time; if it has not, a major and minor loop are generated. The code sample being timed will be the body of this loop. The macro OO closes the compound statement started by the "sufficient time" test, calls endtim, and increments the sample-number index.

The timer1.h header generates a main function which executes all the user's supplied samples until they have all achieved the required minimum amount of time (or until T_MAXITER "maximum iterations" has been reached). The header ends with the opening lines of the definition of a function named t_timeall; the user's timing samples will constitute the body of this function. (See page 9-22 for listing of timer1.h.)

Determining the harness space and time is the job of the calibration program:

```
calib.c:
    /* CALIB - DETERMINE TIME AND SPACE FOR HARNESS */
    #include "timer1.h"
        extern int calibrun;
        register int reg1;
        double d1;

        calibrun = 1;    /* this is a calibration run */

        DO_STMT("no asst") {;} OD
        DO_IEXPR("reg asst") reg1 OD
        DO_FEXPR("dbl asst") d1 OD
```

This resembles a typical timing file, except that the variable calibrun is set to indicate that this is a calibration run, so that begintim does not attempt to locate any file of previously-computed harness parameters. The output of calib needs to be put into a file named parms.dat, so that begintim can read the harness parameters at the start of each timing run.

Two utility functions are used at various places. The error function accepts two string arguments, prints them on stderr, and exits.

```
error:
    /* error - print error message and exit
     */
    #include <stdio.h>
    error(s1, s2)
        char s1[], s2[];
        {
        fprintf(stderr, "%s %s\n", s1, s2);
        fflush(stderr);
        exit(1);
        }
```

The fround function accepts a double argument x (of which only n digits are significant), and formats it into a string, in fixed-point notation with p digits after the decimal. The address of the string is the returned value.

```
fround:
    /* fround - round double x to precision p, n significant digits
     * uses static string for result - not re-entrant
     * fround is an accomodation for K+R-level printf which lacks %.*e or %g
     * slow, fat version - uses sprintf
     */
    #include <stdio.h>
    char *fround(x, p, n)
        double x;
        short p;
        short n;
        {
        double y;
        double log10();
        short digs;
        short nlog;
        static char s[40] = {0};
        char fmt[20];

        sprintf(fmt, "%%.%de", n-1);
        sprintf(s, fmt, x);
        sscanf(s, "%lf", &y);
        if (y == 0)
            nlog = 0;
        else
            nlog = log10(y);
        if (nlog < 0)
            --nlog;
        digs = n - nlog - 1;
        if (digs < 0)
            digs = 0;
        else if (digs > p)
            digs = p;
        sprintf(fmt, "%%.%df", digs);
        sprintf(s, fmt, y);
        if (digs == 0)
            strcat(s, ".");
        while (digs++ < p)
            strcat(s, " ");
        return (s);
        }
    #ifdef TRYMAIN
    main()
        {
        short m;

        for (m = 1; m <= 5; ++m)
            printf("fround(123.57, 2, %d) = %s;\n", m, fround(123.57, 2, m));
        for (m = 1; m <= 5; ++m)
            printf("fround(.013579, 5, %d) = %s;\n", m, fround(.013579, 5, m));
        }
    #endif
```

Installing the Suite

We will indicate the installation process with the outline for a shell script, Make-file, batch file, or whatever technique is available on your system:

1. Compile `begint.c, cputim.c, returnp.c, fround.c, error.c` into an object-code library which we will call `libtim`.

2. Compile `calib.c`, linking it with `libtim`, to produce an executable which we will call `calib.x`.

3. Run `calib.x`, redirecting its standard output into a file named `parms.dat`.

This completes the installation process.

Running a Timing Sample

A timing sample is a source file (`sample.c`, say) that starts by including `timer1.h`, and provides a series of invocations of the `DO...OD` macro combinations, as shown earlier. You need to compile `sample.c` and link it with `libtim` to produce an executable program named `sample.x` (for example). Then run `sample.x`, and its standard output will produce a table of code size in bytes and execution time in microseconds for each of the samples in the file.

The actual coding and execution of a timing sample is as simple as we could make it. All the messy details of the suite itself evolved in an ongoing effort to make the end result easy.

[2-4] Wait States and the 68000 Results

If your machine has something other than one wait state (like ours did), there are some complications to applying the results. When an instruction requires a bus access (for data or instruction bytes), the number of wait states is added to the basic four cycle timing. Thus, for instructions that take little internal execution time, a machine with W wait states will operate at a rate equal to $4/(4+W)$ times the speed of a machine with the same clock rate and no wait states. Therefore, for relatively quick instructions (e.g., increment), our machine is equivalent in speed to a machine with a clock rate of 8 MHz and no wait states, or a 12 MHz machine with two wait states. Some instructions (such as multiply or divide) take a large number of machine cycles to execute, without making any references to the memory for either more instruction bytes or data bytes. For these instructions, the wait states are almost irrelevant; our machine executes divides almost as fast as a 10

MHz machine with no wait states, or any other number of wait states.

To put all of this into simple formulas, let us say that your machine has a clock rate c (MHz) with w wait states. Suppose further that our table shows time T for a given instruction. If the instruction is very quick, you would expect your machine to take (C/(8+2*W))*T microseconds. If the instruction is very slow, you would expect it to take (C/10)*T microseconds.

[7-1] The qsortm Harness

This is the program that we used to time the execution of the qsort function. It makes use of the cputim function, but is otherwise independent of the rest of the timing suite.

```
qsortm.c:
    /* qsortm - test the qsort function */
    #include "local.h"
    #include "cputim.h"
    static long n_compares = 0;
    static int a[10000] = {0};
    /* intcmp - compare two ints */
    int intcmp(pi, pj)
        register int *pi, *pj;
        {
        ++n_compares;
        if (*pi < *pj)
            return (-1);
        else if (*pi == *pj)
            return (0);
        else
            return (1);
```

```
/* qsortm (main) - run the test */
main(ac, av)
    int ac;
    char *av[];
    {
    int i;
    int lim;
    double nlogn;
    double tim; /* in usec */
    cputim_t cputim();

    lim = atoi(av[1]);
    printf("lim=%d\n", lim);
    for (i = 0; i < lim; ++i)
        a[i] = rand();
    printf("start:\n");
    cputim();
    qsort((data_ptr)a, lim, sizeof(int), intcmp);
    tim = 1e6 * (double)cputim() / CLOCK_TICKS_PER_SECOND;
    printf("cpu time = %.3f (sec)\n", tim / 1e6);
    nlogn = lim * log((double)lim) / log(2.);
    printf("n_compares = %ld\n", n_compares);
    printf("cpu time = %.3f (usec) per compare\n", tim / n_compares);
    printf("log N = %.3f\n", log((double)lim) / log(2.));
    printf("N log N = %.3f\n", nlogn);
    printf("cpu time = %.2f N log N (usec)\n", tim / nlogn);
    printf("ratio of n_compares to N log N = %.3f\n\n", n_compares / nlogn);
    for (i = 0; i < lim-1; ++i)
        if (a[i] > a[i+1])
            error("bad value", "");
    exit(0);
    }
```

[9-1] The timer1.h Header

```
timer1.h:
    /* timer1.h - this file is to be included at the front of each
     * timing sample file.
     * Note: variables visible to the sample file all start with "t_";
     * macro names all start with "T_", to avoid name conflicts.
     */
    #include <stdio.h>

    #define void int     /* remove if compiler supports  void */
    typedef int bool;
    #define T_NO  0
    #define T_YES 1
    #define T_MAXITER  10000000

    #define T_SKIP 0
    #define T_NOASST 1
    #define T_REGASST 2
    #define T_DBLASST 3
    #define T_LOOPDOWN(a, b) for (a = (b)+1; --a > 0;  )
    #define DO_SKIP(S) \
        t_s=S; \
        t_type = T_SKIP; \
        begintim(0); \
        if (0) {
    #define DO_STMT(S) \
        t_s=S; \
        t_type = T_NOASST; \
        if (t_sample[t_try] < t_minsam) { \
        begintim(0); \
        T_LOOPDOWN(t_major, t_majrlim) T_LOOPDOWN(t_minor, t_minrlim)
    #define DO_FEXPR(S) \
        t_s=S; \
        t_type = T_DBLASST; \
        if (t_sample[t_try] < t_minsam) { \
        begintim(0); \
        T_LOOPDOWN(t_major, t_majrlim) T_LOOPDOWN(t_minor, t_minrlim)  t_dbl =
    #define DO_IEXPR(S) \
        t_s=S; \
        t_type = T_REGASST; \
        if (t_sample[t_try] < t_minsam) { \
        begintim(0); \
        T_LOOPDOWN(t_major, t_majrlim) T_LOOPDOWN(t_minor, t_minrlim)  t_reg =
    #define OD ;} endtim(0);  ++t_try;
```

```
/* external references */
extern char *t_s;           /* description of this try */
extern long t_reps;         /* number of samples this iteration */
extern short t_try;         /* which trial number is being done next */
extern short t_type;        /* selection of timing method */
extern double t_minsam;     /* desired minimum samples */
extern double t_sample[];   /* actual samples for each try */
extern char *t_title[];     /* array of descriptions for printout */
extern short t_size[];      /* array of code sizes in bytes */
extern double t_ctime[];    /* array of actual times */

/* static (internal) definitions */
static double t_dbl = 0;        /* target for forced double assigns */
static unsigned t_majrlim = 0;  /* major loop limit */
static unsigned t_major = 0;    /* major loop variable */
static unsigned t_minrlim = 0;  /* minor loop limit */
static unsigned t_minor = 0;    /* minor loop variable */
static void t_timeall();
main()
    {
    bool more;
    short i;

    t_reps = 1;
    do
        {
        t_try = 0;
        if (t_reps <= 10000)
            {
            t_minrlim = t_reps;
            t_majrlim = 1;
            }
        else
            {
            t_minrlim = 10000;
            t_majrlim = t_reps / 10000;
            }
        t_timeall();
        t_reps *= 10;
        more = T_NO;
        for (i = 0; i < t_try; ++i)
            if (t_sample[i] < t_minsam)
                more = T_YES;
        } while (more && t_reps <= T_MAXITER);
    report();
    }
static void t_timeall()
    {
    register int t_reg;     /* target for forced assigns */
    /* ... USER'S FUNCTION CONTINUES HERE ... */
```

BIBLIOGRAPHY

Bentley, Jon Louis **[1982]**. *Writing Efficient Programs*. Prentice-Hall, 1982.

Bentley, Jon Louis **[1984a]**. "How to Sort." *Communications of the ACM*. Vol 27, No 4, April 1984, Pp 287-291.

Bentley, Jon Louis **[1984b]**. "Squeezing Space." *Communications of the ACM*. Vol 27, No 5, May 1984, Pp 416-421.

Brooks, Frederick P. **[1975]**. *The Mythical Man-Month*. Addison-Wesley, 1975.

Hoare, Charles Antony Richard **[1981]**. "The Emperors's Old Clothes," (1980 ACM Turing Award Lecture), *Communications of the ACM*. February 1981, Volume 24, Number 2, Pages 75-83.

Kernighan, Brian W., and P. J. Plauger **[1981]**. *Software Tools in Pascal*. Addison-Wesley, 1981.

Knuth, Donald E. **[1973]**. *The Art of Computer Programming. Volume I: Fundamental Algorithms. (Second Edition)*. Addison-Wesley, 1973.

Linderman, J. P. **[1984]**. "Theory and Practice in the Construction of a Working Sort Routine." *AT&T Bell Laboratories Technical Journal*. Vol 63, No 8, October 1984, Pp 1827-1843.

Piper, Watty. **[1979]**. *The Little Engine That Could*. Scholastic Press, 1979.

Plum, Thomas **[1983]**. *Learning to Program in C*. Plum Hall, 1983.

Plum, Thomas **[1984]**. *C Programming Guidelines*. Plum Hall, 1984.

Plum, Thomas **[1985]**. *Reliable Data Structures in C*. Plum Hall, 1985.

Smith, Bob, and Tom Puckett, **[1984]**. "Life in the Fast Lane: Techniques for Obtaining Timing Information with Microsecond Resolution on the PC." *PC Tech Journal*. April 1984, Pp 62-74.

INDEX

PLUM HALL

1 Spruce Av Cardiff NJ O8232
609-927-3770

REPLY FORM

Efficient C

Please check all that apply:

_____ I would like to be notified of any revisions to the ANSI standard for C which affect the content of this book, or of any corrections to the book.

_____ I would like to report an error, suggest an improvement, etc:

NAME _____

COMPANY _____

ADDRESS _____

_____

CITY _____ STATE _____ ZIP _____

COUNTRY _____

PHONE _____

Plum Hall Inc
1 Spruce Avenue
Cardiff NJ 08232 USA